PXXS

300

S0-BNI-578

SEX GODDESSES OF THE SILENT SCREEN

SEX GODDESSES OF THE SILENT SCREEN

NORMAN ZIEROLD

Henry Regnery Company • Chicago

Library of Congress Cataloging in Publication Data

Zierold, Norman J
   Sex goddesses of the silent screen.

   CONTENTS: The wickedest woman in the world: Theda
Bara.—The too-beautiful girl: Barbara Lamarr.—The wildcat: Pola
Negri. [etc.]
   1. Moving-picture actors and actresses—Biography. I. Title.
PN1998.A2Z55   791.43'028'0922   72-11191

*For his help in gathering the photographs for this
book, the author wishes to thank Kenneth G.
Lawrence of the Memorabilia Shop, Los Angeles,
California. Studio identification for the films from
which stills have been used is indicated in the text.*

Copyright © 1973 by Norman Zierold. All rights reserved.
Published by Henry Regnery Company, 114 West Illinois Street,
   Chicago, Illinois 60610
Manufactured in the United States of America
Library of Congress Catalog Card Number: 72-11191

FOR JEFF AND MARK WOLF

CONTENTS

 INTRODUCTION

Society honors many people for many reasons: craftsmen for their skills, scholars for their intelligence, public leaders for their vision. Awards are given for achievement in the arts and sciences, and citations recognize sterling traits of character. But applause and riches sometimes go to young women simply because they have what is known as sex appeal, because they are considered beautiful, alluring, seductive. Neither the mind nor the character but the flesh draws men to them. They are the sex goddesses, and their lot is not an easy one.

Beauty, the very quality that forms the basis of their attraction, is hopelessly elusive and evanescent. Beauty is nothing without a beholder, and the beholder keeps changing his taste. One day bobbed hair is in, the next day out; blondes reign for a time before the fashion shifts to brunettes or redheads; bosoms rise to splendid heights and then an arbitrary mode flattens them with the ruthless power of a steamroller. In her time, the fleshy writhings and wild looks of Theda Bara were considered sensually arousing; today they would be looked on as camp. Clara Bow admitted that she never really knew what "It"

ix

meant. It was painfully obvious, however, when "It" no longer registered with the public, and her career was over.

If times were often difficult, they were never dull for these silent screen sex goddesses. They were helping to launch a glamorous new industry. In the popular imagination they were accorded the status of royalty. Their lives, accordingly, were supercharged on every level, as extraordinary as the melo-dramatic epics in which they starred. In the choices made for this book the author's preferences inevitably figure. None-theless, it could be argued that the selection is representative of the period of the teens and the twenties — with Mae Murray the silent era's leading blonde siren, Clara Bow the sauciest redhead, and three dark-haired vampires, a just proportion since bru-nettes dominated the vampire field. Theda Bara, who brought the term vamp into common usage, is an obvious choice. The brief, poignant, almost delirious life of Barbara LaMarr assures her of a place. And Pola Negri is a wonderfully apt symbol of flamboyant Hollywood in its heyday. While the space accorded Gloria Swanson, in the Negri chapter, is relatively brief, it should be noted that Queen Gloria was one-third siren but two-thirds leading lady: she was known as the Clotheshorse, and this book is devoted to women who wore as few clothes as possible. Other favorites, while also not granted separate chapters, are treated in the concluding pages.

SEX GODDESSES OF THE SILENT SCREEN

1

THEDA BARA

THE
WICKEDEST
WOMAN
IN THE
WORLD

It was a cold winter evening in early March, 1918. During the day, newspapers in Omaha, Nebraska, had printed disheartening figures of American casualties on the European battlefronts, and by afternoon an icy blizzard was sweeping the city, adding physical discomfort to mental anguish. Neither the war news nor bad weather, however, could keep the Women's Club of Omaha from holding its monthly meeting. There was business to be done, urgent business. Theda Bara was on the loose once more, undulating her shameful serpentine way through the new William Fox version of *Cleopatra*, and if the club's Better Films Committee could not protect the entire nation from her wiles, it could at least protect Omaha.

Mrs. C.W. Hayes, presiding, had scarcely called the meeting to order before the criticism began. "I'm here to tell you, *Cleopatra* is not fit for children to see," shouted a woman in the back of the room as she wriggled out of her snow-frosted overcoat. "Shut up the movies and keep the children at home," another voice snapped. "We can't have Sunday school any more — so many children go to the movies on that day," said Nellie

3

Magee, a mission worker. "If the movies interfere with church attendance, bring movies into the church," declared Mrs. E. G. Bailey. "They're here to stay, so let us use them to the best advantage." The remark brought a fiery outcry from the audience, to which the presiding officer added fuel by saying, "People won't listen to dry sermons. I don't like them myself. If we can't close the movies on Sunday, let's have Bible study films that day. I just love the movies."

In the ensuing hubbub a timid voice suggested that *Cleopatra* had value as history, but a chorus of dissent spoke of its "wicked, suggestive" nature. "I must confess to being shocked at the movements of the actress," said one of the few men in the room. "She was certainly Hooverizing on clothes," said a woman at his side. "Put on *your* best clothes every Sunday morning and go to church, and you won't have to worry about your children going astray," said Dr. Jennie Callfas.

"Many clubwomen send their children to the movies every night in order that they may fill social engagements," Mrs. Jerome Lillie declared disapprovingly. "Go to the producers and censor films before they are released," said Mrs. J.H. Dumont, adding a bit of solid midwestern wisdom: "Don't lock the barn after the horse is stolen." "Moving picture men are not at fault, but the public is," said Mrs. D.G. Craighead. "Managers give the public what it demands. Films not fit for children should not be witnessed by grown-ups. Now take *Cleopatra* . . ."

At the end of the spirited meeting the Better Films Committee took a vote and decided that Theda Bara in *Cleopatra* was fit neither for children nor for adults. The widely publicized condemnation had one immediate result: an unprecedented demand for tickets to the film, which was sold out for its entire Omaha engagement. Throughout the Midwest similar good fortune greeted the Theda Bara super-production.

By coincidence, Winfield Sheehan, General Manager of the Fox Corporation, happened to be in Omaha a few days after the meeting. Despite the frigid climate, he radiated warmth. "If the women condemn a picture, they are right," he declared. "The women are always right. It makes no difference to me what they do or say, they are right. They are beautiful — and they are right."

Sheehan went on to say that if Cleopatra had lived in Omaha during the recent snowstorm, she might well have worn furs to face the streets. It should be remembered, however, that Cleo, alias Theda Bara, was not in a blizzard but in more balmy surroundings. Still, of course, the women were right.

For more than three years, in a proliferating series of meetings across the land, outraged women had put the burgeoning film medium on trial, just as a half century later their grandchildren were to debate the baneful influence of television on their homes. With a war raging in Europe they found time to worry about violence and gore and Wild West escapades at the neighborhood theater. But most of all they worried about Theda Bara, the Vampire, the Wickedest Woman in the World, as the Fox organization gleefully billed her.

St. Augustine had said there was little merit to resisting temptation unless you had experienced it. The multitudes who went to see the Vampire were confirmed, if unknowing, Augustinians. Most of them were also unaware that the object of their co-mingled hate and love was the first full-scale product of filmdom's newly founded publicity mills. The prefabrication, the hoax, was of such magnitude that even today the name of Theda Bara is symbolic of fatal feminine charm.

Godfather to the legend was William Fox, a former cloth sponger turned penny arcade proprietor and film exhibitor. In 1914 Fox decided to turn producer. His first film, *Life's Shop Window*, was made on Staten Island at a cost of $4,500. Somewhat more went into *A Fool There Was*, the outdoor scenes for which were filmed in Florida. Because the leading woman was an unknown, the advance publicity concentrated on the male star, Edward Jose, who had played on stage opposite Sarah Bernhardt. When the film was released, in January, 1915, Jose was praised for his performance, but the uproar over the interpretation of the female lead reached hysterical proportions. The fantastic fame and infamy of Theda Bara were literally created overnight.

"As the Vampire, Theda Bara gives the woman not one redeeming feature, her only appeal being purely animal," wrote the *New York Morning Telegraph*. "She is imperious, a fury, a perfect volcano of conflicting emotions. The only real pleasure she gets out of life seems to be in inflicting pain and anguish upon foe and friend alike. It is quite the most revolting but fascinating character that has appeared upon the screen for some time. Magnificent gowns — and an occasional lack of them — add greatly to the forcefulness of Miss Bara's work."

"Miss Bara misses no chance for sensuous appeal in her portrayal of the Vampire," wrote the *New York Dramatic Mirror*. "She is a horribly fascinating woman, vicious to the core, and cruel. When she says, 'Kiss me, my fool,' the fool is generally ready to obey and enjoy a prolonged moment, irrespective of the less enjoyable ones to follow."

From regional papers came every variation of extravagant praise. "Theda Bara was an instant triumph in the role of the vampire woman," said the *San Francisco Call & Post*; and the *Pittsburgh Leader* proclaimed, "Miss Bara's interpretation is remarkable for intense dramatic realism, while her wonderfully seductive beauty serves to enhance the illusion created by her art."

So powerful was the fledgling star's characterization that it soon added new words to the everyday vocabulary. "Vampire," said the dictionary, is "a woman who preys upon men. To vamp: to prey upon men, entice, inveigle, captivate."

While history had provided numerous prototypes for the vampire, it was a nineteenth-century painting by Sir Edward Burne-Jones that was the immediate ancestor. In a remarkable portrait the Victorian master had tried to show the soul, or lack of soul, in the face of a woman who takes all and gives nothing in return, who squeezes everything out of a man and leaves a desiccated rind. The work had inspired Rudyard Kipling to write an unflattering poem about the female of the species called "The Vampire," which began with the lines:

> *A fool there was and he made his prayer—*
> *(Even as you and I)*
> *To a rag and a bone and a hank of hair—*
> *(We called her the woman who did not care)*
> *But the fool he called her his lady fair—*
> *(Even as you and I)*

In 1909 Porter Emerson Browne knocked out a melodrama that took its title from the first line of Kipling's poem. With Robert Hilliard playing the fool and Katharine Kaelred his tormentor, it enjoyed a ready success on the legitimate stage before its transfer to the screen. There Theda Bara made the "rag and a bone and a hank of hair" a pretty harsh description of a woman, forever her own.

Before an invited audience at the Strand Theater in New York, the first showing of *A Fool There Was* was preceded by the recitation of Kipling's poem. Even the cynical verse could not adequately prepare the house for the scenario about to unfold, the story of a neurotic woman gone mad, a woman with enough sex appeal to supply the needs of an entire town and with a temperament that allowed the prodigal use of it, never to good purpose. To come into contact with the Vampire was like touching the third rail, resulting in a swift demise or grotesque maiming. All along the track one could see or hear her victims, some already dead, others begging in the streets, still others finishing off her work with bullets through their own brains.

Early in the film the audience learned of a youth who commits suicide because the Vampire deserts him in favor of John Schuyler, the pathetic "hero" of *A Fool There Was.* The affair with Schuyler, a married man, starts on an ocean liner and continues abroad under the romantic skies of Italy. Alternating with languorous tableaux and scenes of unleashed passion are sequences showing this latest fool's wife and child at home in America: pathos and even comic relief are supplied by his little girl. Completely dominated by the wanton woman, Schuyler returns with her to New York, where his physical and moral degeneration continues despite the efforts of friends to drag him out of the quicksand of the Vampire's lips. As Kipling's poem put it,

So some of him lived but the most of him died—
(Even as you and I)

"There are such women, plenty of them. I have made an especial study of the type," Theda Bara afterward confided to the press, which was to find her an unfailing source of lively copy for the next four years. One of her observations on the vampire type of woman was that despite a popular view that saw wicked women as dark beauties, brunettes — like her — were less cold-hearted and calculating than blondes when they developed into vampires. In blondes there could be found a substratum of hardness and heartlessness which was appalling, said Theda.

"My conception of the vampire character is not so much of a woman as it is of a youthful symbol of sin," she went on. "She is afraid of nothing except old age and death. Her heart is a charnel house of men's dead hopes and withered ambitions. She thrives on the deaths. This vampire of mine possesses only one good or decent quality, her courage. Some night when she faces old age and her mirror shows her wrinkles, she will pass out. Gas or poison, I should think. But nothing that would disfigure her. Such is my conception of the woman who wrought the fool's undoing."

The Fox organization was not fully prepared for the breath-taking leap of their new star's popularity. Since no vehicle was immediately available for her talents, she was cast in a film based on Tolstoy's *The Kreutzer Sonata*, which starred the much-admired dramatic actress Nance O'Neil. The Bara role had her playing a beautiful and ruthlessly passionate girl who without scruples breaks the heart of her sister Miriam so that she may possess Miriam's husband, a brilliant violinist.

Never again was Theda Bara to share star billing with a woman. With *The Clemenceau Case*, still early in 1915, she settled into a mold that was to hug her well-rounded form for endless reels. Based on a play by the younger Dumas, author of *Camille,* the film was directed by Herbert Brenon: stage actor William Shay was cast as Pierre Clemenceau and Stuart Holmes as his best friend, Ritz Constantin. As the beautiful but wicked Iza, Theda Bara was out to avenge wrongs supposedly done to her sex by men. Following a long train of victims were Pierre, whom she lured into marriage, and Ritz Constantin. The final scene of the film was so characteristic that it deserves elaboration.

In her luxurious and exotic boudoir the restless Iza tries to find distraction. For a few moments she toys with a giant king python but tires of it and puts it aside, easing herself languidly onto an ottoman lounge. Here she awaits the coming of Pierre, who, unbeknownst to her, has learned of her affair with his friend Ritz. When Pierre arrives, Iza throws her arms about his neck and drags him down beside her. As their lips meet, they hear the sound of a key in the locked door. Ritz Constantin dashes in, looks wildly about, and with a savage oath rushes at Iza — who laughs cruelly at his distraction. Suddenly her beautiful face becomes horribly contorted, and her lips let out a fearful scream. In the moment of their clinging embrace Pierre has seized a jeweled dagger from the wall close to his hand and has plunged the blade deep into her heart. His own life has been ruined, but he still has the courage to save his friend from a similar fate. The vampire is dead in her lair. As her limp body falls back on the blood-splattered draperies, Pierre goes calmly over to the telephone. "Sergeant, send up your man. I have just killed my wife," says the film's melodramatic final caption.

Death was a suitable punishment for Iza Clemenceau, but filmgoers knew that Theda Bara lived, that her menace was likely to grow. William Fox knew it too, and he made sure that it grew at the fastest possible pace, on screen and off. He fabricated a vampire symbol that took its hold on the public and helped to characterize an era.

Among his major assets in these endeavors were the immense physical appeal of his star and her lively, pliant mentality. By her fans Theda Bara was considered strangely, sensually, exotic-ally, perversely beautiful. Large black hypnotic eyes were her most salient feature. Makeup men set them in heavy Kohl-like frames within a rounded dead-white face. Dark lustrous hair was at times left to trail in great waves over bare shoulders, at others contained within black spit curls, and on still other occasions was tucked behind elaborate headgear that ran the gamut from peacock feathers to jeweled crowns. Hoop earrings became a Bara trademark, as did bronze spangles, the leopard-skin couch, the tiger-skin rug, and the long gold cigarette holder.

The Vampire's generously voluptuous frame seldom moved to an ordinary rhythm. Rather it glided, slinked, undulated, its lush curves displayed in diaphanous gowns or filmy shawls. Low necks and soft slithery satins were much in evidence. A veil or two and a few festoons of synthetic pearls were often ample costume for the bosomy, sultry-eyed Theda. A sinister droop to the left eye and a cruel expression of the mouth appeared when the vampire was about to strike.

No woman so calculatingly seductive, so alluringly cruel, so wonderfully wicked could possibly be of American origin. Theda Bara was a love pirate, a sex bitch. She could be French perhaps, or Oriental, but certainly not American. Even before the cameras had started rolling for *A Fool There Was*, William Fox realized that the female lead could certainly not be named Theodosia Goodman. Twenty-five-year-old Theodosia had her-self pondered the matter and came forth with a new name. Theda was a contraction of her first name and Bara was the family name of her maternal grandfather, who was Swiss.

There still remained the matter of a birthplace. Once again the truth was of no help. Theda Bara could not be born in Cincinnati, Ohio. Nice little Jewish girls from the Midwest did not become vampires! Fox turned to his publicity department for help and under the aegis of a henchman named Goldfarp — who had not felt it necessary to change *his* name — the Bara myth was launched.

"Prominent actress imported from Paris," said the *Exhibitors Bulletin* in announcing the casting of Theda Bara in *A Fool*

There Was. "Director Frank Powell was confronted by a problem. He needed an actress of scope and ability to play a woman
who lures a man to dissipation and finally to a degrading death
in her arms. . . . Powell recalled a girl he had seen at the Théâtre
Antoine, an actress who fulfilled absolutely the type he
required."

"Purely Gallic in type," wrote the Philadelphia *North
American*, picking up the Fox publicity weavings: "A French
actress of personal distinction and undeniable fascination." A
San Francisco daily hardly bothered to rephrase the Goldfarp
invention. "In Paris there is a theatre called the Théâtre
Antoine. That is its official name, but so different are the performances given there from the general, everyday sort of plays,
that the public have nicknamed it the 'Playhouse of Thrills.'
That this theater must have a cast of actors above the ordinary
goes without saying, and the brightest star is Theda Bara, the
beautiful and brilliantly gifted leading lady. . . ."

In point of fact, Mlle. Goodman had made her first stage
performance in the suburbs of Cincinnati in 1898. At the age of
seven she recited "The Dirty-Faced Brat," a maudlin piece
about a starving boy who goes out to shovel snow in the bitter
cold to earn money for food. The exhibition took place in a
neighbor's barn to which her brother had lured a youthful
audience with promises of lemonade and cookies and threats of
reprisal for nonattendance.

After a relatively normal childhood, including public school,
a year with a tutor, and a term at a girl's college,
eighteen-year-old Theodosia — called "Teddy" and "Theda" by
her friends — made up her mind to become an actress, although
her studies had emphasized music. Reluctantly her father paid
her way to New York, where she moved into a small hotel near
Washington Square. Failing to land a Broadway role, she
accepted a small part in a road company at $25 a week. When
the company manager threatened to cut that meager sum to
$18, the disillusioned young actress returned to Washington
Square. The Great White Way still paid her no mind.

After several years of intense personal and professional disappointment, the prospect of performing in a Greek drama led her to Europe. The project collapsed. Despite ill health, she joined an obscure open-air company that performed bad Shakespeare around the English countryside. Just before the outbreak of World War I she returned to New York, slender, pale, sad-eyed. She was about to become the Vampire, but she didn't look like one.

Little did it matter. Theda Bara was being created out of whole cloth, along with her pedigree: "Theda Bara was born in 1891 in Egypt — in the shadow of the Sphinx. She was the daughter of a French painter and an Arabian princess, who had eloped to an oasis in the Sahara."

A number of variations on this theme of exotic parenthood and birthplace were circulated, one by Louella Parsons, writing at the time for the *Chicago Herald.* "Theda Bara," wrote Louella, "is the daughter of Giuseppe Bara, one of the foremost sculptors of the modern school. Her mother is Theda de Lysie, one of the best-known of the French emotional actresses. As a young girl Mlle. Bara studied painting with her father as pre-ceptor. Later she joined her mother in classic drama, playing vampire roles at the Théâtre Antoine, where she was seen by director Frank Powell, who remembered her when casting *A Fool There Was.*"

The press tales became even more confused. One provided her with a Russian grandmother whose blithe seductiveness had devastated most of Europe. Another said that she had a Bourbon nose, the legacy of a royal French ancestor. As Belgium was overrun by German armies, Theda's press agents reported that she was "proud of a trace of Belgian blood. She has concentrated her affections, her pity, and her charities upon the war sufferers of the tiny kingdom which was the first and weakest of the nations stricken by the great war."

The Arabian background was given a happy fillip when it was discovered that Bara was an anagram of Arab. There was proof of Theda's exotic origins.

In reality, Bernard Goodman, Theodosia's father, was a reasonably well-to-do middle-class Jewish businessman, born in

Chorsel, Poland. His wife was born Pauline Bara de Coppet in La Chaux de Fonds, Switzerland. Theodosia was named after Theodosia Burr, the lovely but ill-fated daughter of Aaron Burr. A sister, Esther, and a brother, Marque, completed the family. With Theda's success, all the Goodmans changed their name to the more famous Bara. None, however, was a painter or sculptor or princess. Nor did Theda enter American films direct from glorious European triumphs, as her publicity had it.

Europe had, in fact, been a dismal experience for the young actress, and on her return, New York provided further disappointments. Money at her small apartment was running low the day a man approached Theda in the street and timidly said that he was an agent for motion pictures. Her eyes had caught his attention, he said. He felt she would photograph well. He could get her a job at $175 a week. Recovering from the shock of the encounter, Theda haughtily informed him that she despised the idiotic young film medium and would not go into the movies even for a million.

Another year of poverty followed, climaxed by a fire in her apartment and a tiring battle with the insurance company, which finally paid $900 on a $2,000 policy. Opportunity now beckoned again. Director Frank Powell of Fox Pictures became acquainted with Theda and asked her to watch him direct. When he offered her the female lead in *A Fool There Was*, the worn-out girl swallowed her pride and accepted with stoic distaste.

If *A Fool There Was* gave a clear-cut definition of Theda Bara as a death-dealing, smouldering-eyed screen vampire, a home-wrecker to end all home-wreckers, William Fox, his man Goldfarp, and their lackeys poured out to the press a word portrait of Theda Bara that was easily as exaggerated and outlandish as her screen portrayals. For the next four years, Theodosia Goodman was the accomplice, the beneficiary, and to a considerable extent, the victim of this high-powered exploitation.

The Clemenceau Case had made everyone's work easy, arousing both institutions and individuals. "Were the National Board of Censorship possessed of any judgement whatsoever, this is the kind of a picture it should place the ban of its disapproval upon," wrote one critic, so upset that he ended his sentence with a preposition. Many local boards did issue edicts of disapproval. A female correspondent, one of an incipient avalanche, wrote bitterly to Theda: "It is such women as you who break up happy homes." From Theda came a reply: "I am working for my living, dear friend, and if I were the kind of woman you seem to think I am, I wouldn't have to." Protests were in vain. The screen Theda made her viewers hate her, and the hatred reached beyond the screen.

After a thorough rehearsal in the publicity department, the new star granted an interview to reporter Nixola Greeley-Smith, which capitalized on the venom generated against her, refuting the charges but at the same time giving them fresh grounds. Wrote Greeley-Smith: "She denies that she is a vampire herself, but her life has not been without its vampire incidents. A few years ago a young man killed himself in his dressing room because she spurned his love. He was furiously jealous of an East Indian Gaekwar then visiting in Paris, who had given the actress a wonderfully wrought snake-bracelet containing an Indian poison. Mlle. Bara was showing the young man the secret spring by which the poison was released from the mouth of the hollow gold snake when he suddenly seized it from her and, placing the snake to his lips, died at her feet!"

The philosophy of the vampire came under scrutiny in this interview, but the prep session with Goldfarp had left Theda fully prepared. "You ask me why men feel as they do about the vampire, what her power is," she said to Greeley-Smith. "If I could tell you that, every woman would be a vampire, and the vampire business would be spoiled. Seriously, I do not know what gives certain women a strange, witch-like power over men. One thing I know: a vampire cannot be fat. There never was and never will be a fat vampire!"

Drifting easily from fat vampires to herself, Theda described herself as "an ordinary woman, a little tall, a little thin, with big black eyes, and a face of shadows." Her own secret power came from detachment, she declared: "A vampire must never love. I have never loved, and if I ever fall under the spell of a man, I know that my power over men will be gone. Every woman must choose whether she will love or be loved. She cannot hope for both. You know we French people have a proverb that in love there is always one who kisses and one who merely turns the cheek. The vampire is content to turn the cheek. That is why she makes fools of men. But believe me, for every woman vampire, there are ten men of the same type, men who take everything from women — love, devotion, beauty, youth — and give nothing in return! V stands for Vampire, and it stands for Vengeance. The vampire that I play is the vengeance of my sex upon its exploiters. You see, I have the face of a vampire, perhaps, but the heart of a *feministe.*"

It was the face of the Vampire that a young man in the Midwest saw one evening as he returned home and looked at his mother-in-law. Without further ado, he proceeded to do her in, and he was promptly charged with murder. The Fox organization was not displeased when the defendant's lawyer asked that a print of *The Clemenceau Case* be made available for jurors in the case. The defendant had seen the film immediately before committing the felony; it was his lawyer's contention that it had affected his mind, leading him to imitate Pierre Clemenceau in an effort to end his own domestic troubles. The defense plea was not sustained, but one more stroke of the brush was added to the picture of Theda Bara as a destroyer.

Artists of stature were enlisted by Fox to fill out the portrait. Charles Dana Gibson depicted Mlle. Bara as "Sin." "Never have I had a model who impressed me as deeply as Miss Bara," the dutiful Gibson said. Famous magazine illustrator James Montgomery Flagg hewed more closely to the line. "Mlle. Bara is unique," he said. "I do not believe there is another woman like her." He called his picture *The Vampire,* and in it the model was seen in a greenish light, with snake-like coils of hair hanging about a dead-white face in which two burning and passionate eyes glowed with a subdued flame.

"Don't be offended at what I am going to say," cautioned portrait painter Roland Montaigne St. Cyr, "but your face is the most beautifully wicked I have ever seen." The result of his efforts was put on private exhibition in New York. It showed Mlle. Bara's strange beauty illuminated in an unearthly reddish light, with her black hair falling about a white face in tangled coils. The lips blazed a startling scarlet in this colorless countenance, and the eyes held a baleful, brooding light that seemed to lurk in their depths.

Fox, Goldfarp, and company summed it all up by saying, "According to New York artists and sculptors, the most fascinatingly wicked and seductively beautiful face in the world belongs to Mlle. Theda Bara. . . ."

Obviously this was the face to illumine *The Devil's Daughter,* Fox's film version of Gabriel D'Annunzio's *La Giaconda.* The eccentric Italian genius had written his drama for Eleanora Duse, who had toured with it in the United States. In a key scene the Devil's Daughter finds that she has been tricked by a man she loved and trusted. "As this man has done to me," she says, "so will I do henceforth to all men. My heart is ice, my passion consuming fire. Let men beware."

Before Theda incarnated this woman with the scorching lips on the screen's inflammable "silver sheets," she told the world of her relationship with the poet-patriot author: "I first met D'Annunzio when he came to Paris to put on a playlet of his at the Théâtre Antoine. I shall never forget my first impression of him. Dark, piercing eyes, a high-pitched screaming voice, and an air of overwhelming conceit. He carried a small dog and shaded himself from the sun on the boulevard with a rose-colored parasol. His clothes were all pure white, but a scarlet sash about his waist made a vivid splash of color. The playlet he was putting on was a mystic sort of thing with a wicked woman of the world as heroine. Another actress was cast for this character. But as soon as she came on the stage, D'Annunzio shrieked out in his shrill voice that she would not do at all. The actress was furious. She stepped up to the author and gave his face a ringing slap. D'Annunzio merely laughed. Then his eyes fell on me. . . . D'Annunzio insisted that I should play the leading part in his sketch. . . . He declared that if I did not take the part, he would not put on the playlet. As everything from his pen was a drawing card, matters were finally arranged. . . ."

From Italy came word, conveyed by the Fox organization, that Gabriel D'Annunzio had said, "There is no one else on earth who is half serpent and half woman like my Giaconda, except Mlle. Bara." This seemed to leave out Mlle. Duse, but such trivial details could be ignored. The author, it was now stated, had "created" the role for the former leading woman at Paris's theater of thrills, Theda Bara.

Film fans were next exposed to slight chills when news stories told of how the company for *The Devil's Daughter*, on location in St. Augustine, Florida, had gone to the beach only to find sand crabs nipping at their feet. Heading for deep water, Mlle. Bara had fortunately seen the familiar triangular black fins of sharks. A hurried retreat to the sheltering hotel porch had put her out of the monsters' danger.

"Mlle. Bara's facial expression is wonderfully brutal and fiendish," wrote a New York critic of the finished film, "but every movement shows grace and charm." Only Theda Bara could bring off such a combination, evoke that clutch of adjectives.

As she rode to work each morning, Theda mulled over the attitudes of her critics and supporters. In New York a woman strode into a theater and kicked a hole through Theda's face in the lobby poster. She then wrote the star to tell her it was worth $10 to have the satisfaction of that act. "Oh, how I hate you," she ended her charming little note. On another occasion, walking in the evening near her home, Theda entered into conversation with a group of youngsters. On her walk she had taken along an apple, and she offered it to a thin, spindly-legged child of the group. When the little girl looked into her eyes, a look of terror came over her. "It's the Vampire!" she shrieked, and the entire troop fled into the night.

Personal incidents and letters of abuse were piling up. It was at once discomforting and amusing for Theda to read such columns in the papers as the Sunday feature that began: "Is this the wickedest face in the world? Its owner does not deny that it may be, since scientists have said that she is the reincarnation of the world's wickedest women and that their crimes have chiseled the lines of her features. Have the physical attributes of the scheming Delilah, of cruel Lucretia Borgia, of diabolical Elizabeth Bathory — who slew no less than 600 girls and young women so she could bathe daily in their blood and so retain her beauty — fatefully found reincarnation so that the women of this age may see face to face the loathsome depths to which the worst of their sex have descended? Are the souls of these monsters of ancient and medieval times welded with others to form the soul of Mlle. Theda Bara?''

From Emily Vaught, described as a "phrenologist and physiognomist," came a revelation: "Theda Bara belongs to what we term the wide-faced, muscular type of people, whose bones are slender and small and who are governed by the same muscular system as the serpent. They are sinuous like the serpent, and as if the characteristics of a reptile were not enough, they have a feline temperament, deliberately taking pains to inflict suffering on others — and because of their destructiveness as a faculty they have a keen sense, understanding, and appreciation of evil. . . . Never in all my experience as a professional character reader have I gazed into a face portraying such wickedness and evil — such characteristics of the vampire and the sorceress.''

For Theda Bara the atmosphere was becoming oppressive. At the studio she made her pitch. She was tired of being typecast as a villainess. "I want to play a kind-hearted, lovable, human woman," she said and meant it. With trepidation, William Fox put her into the film version of Miss M.E. Braddon's popular novel *Lady Audley's Secret.* Her role was that of an unfortunate young wife whose husband goes away to seek his fortune, leaving a note explaining his movements. A drunken father destroys the note in order to hide the fact that he has stolen the money enclosed with it. Grief-stricken, the wife leaves her child behind and soon finds her affections engaged by a wealthy nobleman.

The conflict is too great, however, and eventually she descends into madness.

Before the results of *Lady Audley's Secret* were in, Fox cast its mellowing star in *The Two Orphans,* based on a classic stage melodrama. Her interpretation of the sympathetic role of Henriette was applauded by the critics. "Tender, bewitching and passionate in turn, her work touched the high-water mark of artistry and furnishes undeniable proof of her extraordinary versatility," wrote one reviewer.

But at the box office people stayed away in droves. Both *Lady Audley's Secret* and *The Two Orphans* were financial flops. William Fox learned from this lesson. Her fans wanted Theda of the Curled Lip, not Theda of the Teardrops. Theda was the woman they loved to hate, a foreign witch! The thing was to cast her as a Spanish gypsy, as Carmen, and let her drive Don Jose off his rocker. And so the William Fox Picture Corporation made *Carmen,* starring Theda Bara.

At the Fort Lee Studio on the west bank of the Hudson, Fox reproduced Seville in stucco at a cost of $30,000, the biggest set yet attempted by the company. From Spain came artist Edward Velasquez to supervise technical and architectural details, such as the exact duplication of the Seville bullfight arena. Colonel Antonio Bravo of the Spanish army was put on the payroll to drill battalions of dragoons. Authentic matadors, picadors, and banderilleros were hired, as well as real gypsies. An Andalusian bull was shipped from Madrid.

More important to the public than elaborate props, set, and the five thousand extras Fox had enlisted for crowd scenes was the fact that rival Metro Pictures was also making its version of *Carmen,* having secured opera singer Geraldine Farrar for the title role. That renowned diva was asked to give the world her view of the part, and she readily obliged.

"Men are like cakes," she said. "The one with the pink icing still in the bottom of the bag always seems more delectable than the one with the green icing out of which you have taken a bite. Carmen is simply the natural woman. She is neither moral nor unmoral. She loves Don José, the dragoon, for a while. Then she tires of him and turns to the more exciting, the less certain, toreador as naturally as a little girl turns from the cake she has sampled, and does not care for particularly, to the unbitten cake still in the bag."

"Are men cakes?" sharply questioned Theda Bara when she elaborated on her *Carmen*. "If they are, even a child knows that too much cake is bad for the complexion, and that the difference between the cake one has nibbled and the cake in the bottom of the bag is principally in the imagination of the cake-eater. Men are bargains, the best of them. Men live in the basement of their beings, and when you love a man, you know you are getting a basement bargain. And when you buy a basement bargain, it is generally marked AS IS. I believe in taking a bargain as you find it and not grumbling over its defects. . . . Carmen knows that a stale emotion is as lacking in charm as a wilted flower. She realizes that when a kiss ceases to be a consecration, it becomes a chore."

With the box-office buildup for the two Carmens proceeding at a highly satisfactory pace, William Fox found additional chores for his star that might give her an edge in the publicity stakes. The matter of Theda Bara's reincarnation had touched a receptive nerve, and *Carmen* offered an ideal occasion for a follow-up.

"The belief that I have lived before and have taken many parts on this world's stage has a strong hold on my imagination," Theda confided to reporters. "The most powerful appeal of any literature I have ever known is the simple verse:

> *Or ever the knightly years were gone*
> *With the old world to the grave,*
> *When I was a king in Babylon*
> *And you were a Christian slave.*

"I once was led to consult a professor of astrology and palmistry. He told me many things which have come true. He told me that his science showed that I had passed through many incarnations, that my soul was many-sided, that it had fallen as

Theda Bara

"The Wickedest Woman in the World" in *A Fool There Was,* 1915.

Theda Bara in the pose of the Vampire in *A Fool There Was.*

Theda Bara gets her man again, in *Carmen,* 1915.

Called a "love pirate" and a "sex bitch,"
Bara was despised by many, who considered
her performances immoral. Shown here is a
still from *Heart and Soul*.

The Vampire turns to Shakespeare. Here she poses for
Romeo and Juliet.

Theda Bara with visitors to the set of *Under Two Flags*. Far right is
Fiorello LaGuardia.

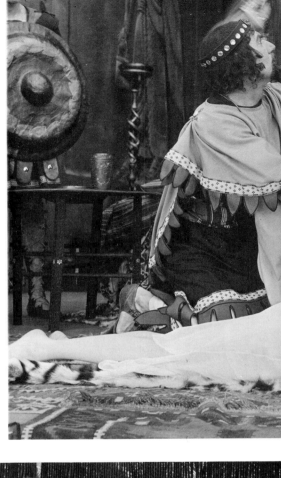

The sensuousness of Bara came to the fore in *Salome,* 1918. Theda tried to absorb "the poetic impulse of Oscar Wilde."

Below left: *Under the Yoke*. Below right: Dot Farley and Theda Bara in *The Unchastened Woman*, 1925.

Bara insisted that she was Cleopatra reincarnated: "I live Cleopatra, I breathe Cleopatra, I *am* Cleopatra!" Above, she and Thurston Hall in *Cleopatra,* 1917.

"The havoc wrought by Theda as a vamp is second only to the European armies," wrote *Variety* of *The Tiger Woman.*

Bara as the Magdalen in *The Forbidden Path,* 1918.

Bara wrote the screenplay of *The Soul of Buddha*, above. She was inspired by the story of Mata Hari.

Bara with Alice Gale in *Her Greatest Love*, 1917.

In mid-1919 Theda persuaded Fox to cast her as the sweet colleen of rhyme and story in *Kathleen Mavourneen*. Golden curls and cotton dresses replaced her usual vampire costume.

Theda Bara at her Hollywood home in 1952.

In costume for *When Men Desire*, 1919, directed by J. Gordon Edwards.

Bara attended a costume party at the home of George Cukor a few weeks before her death, on April 6, 1955.

low as human spirit could fall and also had touched the sun-clad heights. . . ."

The final step in the charade was obvious: "I have felt a strange sensation whenever I have thought of this girl, Carmen, of the Spanish hills. The mere thought of her gives me a thrill. There is now plenty of evidence that Merimee wrote down almost the exact life of the girl Ar Minz, whom he met in Spain, and changed her name on account of family connections. It seems to me that I knew all these events—even before Merimee—that I was Carmen herself!"

Having established the fact that she had lived far in the past as the Spanish smuggler Ar Minz, Fox decided to apply a double whammy and tug at an opposing emotion, the fear of imminent death. "Last night I was looking at the stars again," began the starry-eyed Theda. "I can think of nothing else today, for I read it again and again. Also I read it in the crystal, for there I see not only the past but also the future. Theda Bara will not live long. I am certain of it. I have never lived long. . . . If the world would only know; they will have films of Theda, but Theda will be no more. . . ."

Crystal balls and astrology were not enough. "See," Theda exclaimed fiercely, driving a reporter's surprised forefinger into her little palm, "that's the end of my life-line. I shan't live very long. I find life so wonderful and so varied that I burn myself up always thinking, thinking, thinking."

To give added emphasis to Theda's mournful mullings, her Fox friends gleefully made another morose discovery: Theda was an anagram of Death. It was too good to be true. There wasn't much more to be said about the matter, but the startling facts could be repeated over and over in a happy delirium— Theda Bara respelled was Arab Death!

Anagrams notwithstanding, Theda easily lasted through the filming of *Carmen.* So did Geraldine Farrar, who had no death apprehensions. Both were highly applauded financial block-busters. Farrar, fiery and forceful, vamped Wallace Reid, her Don José, and found that screen favor added to her concert grosses. Elinar Linden, a Scandinavian opera singer being groomed as a rival to Francis X. Bushman, made his American debut as Theda's Don José. In a dramatic climax he watches Carmen close her eyes in death outside the bullring; then astride his horse he leaps to his own destruction from the top of an eighty-five-foot cliff. It was only one of the film's many departures from primary sources.

In her "original, wild, free, untrammeled" version as the heroine, Theda Bara used her rolling eyes, languishing inhalations, and tense, undulating movements to create a vampire at once sensuous, passionate, and fairly groggy with emotion. As an added fillip she smoked modern machine-made Turkish cigarettes, large and oval-shaped, such as Merimee and his Ar Minz certainly never saw.

"She has the science of silent seduction worked out to the nth power," said the *New York Evening Mail*. "By the twinkle of an eyelid and a squirm of the body she has all the gallants in the neighborhood trotting Bara-ward."

"Miss Bara does most of her real acting through a marvelous control of her features," wrote the critic for the *New York Evening Journal*. "Her mouth can express a hundred expressions, her lips are provocative even when they are parted cruelly, her eyes are wistful when they are wicked. There is an intelligent foreign element about this actress that savors of the real thing. . . ."

It was, of course, not the real thing, and in about the middle of the year, still 1915, a number of reporters informed their readers that the exotic Theda was *née* Theodosia Goodman in Cincinnati. One newspaperman cornered Theda and the man who had helped to rewrite her life.

"Were you born in Cincinnati, Miss Bara?" he asked.

"I wonder who circulated that story," Theda replied. "Where was I born, Mr. Goldfarp?"

"Egypt," said Mr. Goldfarp without hesitation.

Not long after, the *New York Times* assumed the task of looking into the matter. A reporter for the *Times* asked the same question. Theda smiled enigmatically. "And what, pray, has that to do with my art?" she inquired. "What does it matter who I am or whence I came? Is it not enough that I am here, with a certain gift, perhaps, for expressing my feelings through the new pantomimic art of the cinema, without knowing about my antecedents? . . . I have the Bourbon nose. My mother was a descendant of the Bourbons. . . . Some say that Bara is Arab spelled backward, but what's in a name?"

The *Times* reporter was not inclined to pursue the matter much further. "The lustrous beauty of the screen apparition glowed brighter in this living presence," he wrote. "It was the rich dark beauty of the Gallic and Oriental races—large dark eyes, black hair, white, evenly matched teeth set in a mouth whose frequent smiles belied the tragedy that lurked in its drooping corners. The head was well-shaped and the profile good, so that . . . the merciless camera would have the utmost difficulty in catching Miss Bara in an unbecoming pose."

As for columnist Wallace Franklin, an ardent admirer, he was candid about his attitude. He knew that Bara was the name of Theda's grandfather and only coincidentally Arab spelled backward, but what of it? "I wish to believe," he wrote. "I am going to believe. I *do* believe that Allah is Allah, and that Bara is Bara, that the ivory angel of purgatory is an Eastern Star, was born under the shadow of the Sphinx, and in physical texture is as bizarre a woof of bloods as she is cosmopolitan in mentality. And I see no reason for disbelieving what it most pleases me to believe."

So much of the world felt this way that William Fox, Goldfarp, and the rest of the team found their job impeded not a whit by the killjoys who turned up from time to time with mundane bits of information about the background of Theda Bara. Some lout was bound to reveal that Theda lived in a sunlit apartment at 500 West End Avenue with her mother, father, brother, and sister. The publicity department effectively countered by informing her admirers that Theda lived alone in Oriental splendor, with only two Moorish servants—in their eighties—to attend to her wants. Let some wily columnist say that Theda was born in Cincinnati or, as one had it, in a cyclone cellar in Kansas. The Fox minions had a story that would quickly turn the item into a discounted rumor.

Sin, Theda's new picture, provided the occasion. Playing a characteristic vampire, she obsesses her fiancé to such a degree that he steals the sacred jewels of the Madonna and lays them at her feet. When she realizes the enormity of her crime, she alternately laughs hysterically and cries, wandering distraught and aimless, finally becoming insane from fright—par for the course for Satan's soulmate, the apostle of sin, the satanic sorceress.

For the part of Rosa in the film, said the Fox press release, Theda personally ransacked the Italian quarter of New York, seeking out authentic period jewelry. After an unsuccessful, wearying day, she was ready to give up when she glanced into the dingy glass window of a basement shop on Mulberry Street. With a shock she recognized a locket which had once been in the family. She rushed inside and found within it a miniature of her father, the locket having been his wedding gift to her mother. Theda recalled that years ago much of her mother's jewelry had been stolen while they were traveling in Italy. Now the cherished heirloom was back in her hands, and with a refreshed heart Theda had cabled the good news to Paris, where her mother—so went the Fox release—was engaged in Red Cross work.

The story was designed to establish the Vampire's European background, and thanks to the countless newspapers that printed it, it did.

After *Sin* Theda made a film version of Bartley Campbell's play *The Galley Slave,* which put her shapely limbs temporarily behind the cruel, demanding oars. Next came *Destruction,* with Theda on the trail of a wealthy manufacturer. As a sybaritic woman oblivious to the methods used to appease her appetites, she stirs up dissension between labor and management. When an angry mob learns that she is the cause of all their troubles, they trace her to a hiding place in her mansion, which accidentally catches fire. Here the plot deals out a measure of poetic justice to Satan's chief recruiting officer, for after she has gone about her own regular job of setting souls on fire, she is herself cast into the flames and forced to remain until she turns into a heap of ashes.

"It proves what her film friends have long feared for Theda," wrote the *New York Evening Mail,* "that she would one day suffer spontaneous combustion and go up in smoke."

Theda Bara's final film in 1915 was entitled *The Serpent,* and in it she writhed and glided and lured and fascinated to her heart's content.

Seldom had even an old-fashioned melodrama carried a plot putting so severe a strain on credulity. Theda Bara fans did not seem to mind. She had made eleven pictures in one year, and "Hell's Handmaiden" was now receiving over 200 letters a day. Effusive poems accompanied many; 1,329 contained offers of marriage. A Sing Sing convict entered into weekly correspondence, in which he said that he was writing a screen play for his idol. Unsolicited scenarios arrived from plumbers, college boys, ministers, and shop girls at the rate of thirty a week. Gifts within the year added up to 1,186 pounds, plus a hundred pounds of candy each month, all donated to hospitals or orphanages. Twelve months earlier no one knew whether Bara was the name of a new toothpaste or a rare malady, but by the end of the year 162 babies had been named after Theda, a number that easily outdistanced those honoring Colonel Theodore Roosevelt, the runner-up.

"Box office receipts from Coney Island to the Golden Gate prove that the public wants her to be a vampire," wrote columnist Archie Bell. "But how long can she keep on the same track?" For the moment, there seemed little cause for apprehension. The *New York Times* made a statistical study of what it called "the flaming comet of the cinema firmament." Of each of Theda's eleven pictures there were forty prints, all constantly in use. In the larger playhouses, three performances a day were the rule, while in the far more numerous smaller theaters, performances were continuous, up to six a day. If the average attendance was tabulated at 200 persons and the average daily performances at five, 400,000 people a day were seeing Theda Bara films. Since these estimates were conservative, a half million was a more likely figure. In a week the Vampire's face thus flashed on the retinas of more than three million fans in a movie-mad world. In a year the staggering figures of 182 million witnessed her celluloid charms.

At the end of 1915 the leading deaf-and-dumb institute in New York voted Theda Bara the most expressive actress on the screen, and a motion picture popularity contest listed the country's favorite female stars in this order: (1) Clara Kimball Young; (2) Anita Stewart; (3) Virginia Norden; (4) Mary Pickford; (5) Theda Bara; (6) Pearl White; (7) Beverly Bayne; (8) Edith Storey; (9) Alice Joyce; (10) Florence La Badie.

Theda had much to be grateful for, but she also had her worries. The women who were frightened of Theda in turn frightened her. To her mind, they completely misunderstood her, failed to grasp what she increasingly viewed as her unique professional mission. "Why do people hate me so?" she asked mournfully. "I try to show the world how attractive sin may be, how very beautiful, so that one must be always on the lookout and know evil even in disguise. I am a moral teacher then. But what is my reward? I am detested."

When the Catholic Federation in her home town made protests to the city against the showing of *The Serpent,* Theda sent a strong admonishing letter to the mayor, the honorable George Puchta. "I cannot conceive how my appearance in pictures in Cincinnati theaters could give grounds for the protests now being published," she began. "Every mother, every minister, every person with the well-being of the younger element of Cincinnati owes me gratitude for what I have accomplished through these pictures. Every picture in which I have appeared has a clear and understandable moral. I have just as definite a place, just as high a mission as the best of your evangelists and the most beloved of your local ministers. Through the silent but expressive medium of the motion picture I am saving hundreds of girls from social degradation and wrong-doing. I believe I am showing time and again the unhappiness and misery that fall to the lot of transgressors, and the contempt and hatred which such people inspire in good society, and among the well-behaved people of the world. Furthermore, I am reaching one million persons each day, an audience larger than was ever had by any man or woman in the world's history."

Today, producers of films with violent content give parallel apologies for presenting their brutal, bloody sagas—that is, seeing violence will turn us away from it.

In her letter Theda went on to decry the nation's prudery. "Why should anyone declaim against the so-called sex drama?" she asked. "Sex is the most vital influence in life. From the time a person is born into the world he is constantly under the influence of sex. When I use the word sex, I use it in its true sense, which is its best sense. Most people give the word sex a false meaning."

Support for Theda's position, albeit with a twist, came from Victor O. Freeburg, Professor of Photoplay at Columbia University. One of the first academics to bear a title relating to the new film industry, Freeburg announced that the screen vampire had a healthy influence on her audiences. "Most girls are good, but good girls do not want to see other good girls upon the screen," he said. "There's no interest, no fascination in that for them. Miss Bara shows something different, vastly different from the life they know. Most moving picture audiences want enjoyment by contrast. Few are either daring enough or desirous enough of leading a vampire existence, but through the medium of Theda Bara they can do her deeds and live her life. Their emotions are enriched by just that much."

In addition to letting the world know that she was doing good, Theda thought that the time had come to separate her screen image from her private person. "I have a heart that longs for the same things that any normal, wholesome woman longs for," she told the press. "To carry out my screen parts I have had to stifle a great many of my little desires. I enjoy things other women enjoy—afternoon teas, spiced with a bit of gossip perhaps, shopping with luncheon in an attractive tearoom. . . ." The thought of a vampire at tea was, of course, ridiculous. Vampires drank absinthe with chloral hydrate on the side. Theda found it hard to keep a straight normal wholesome woman's face as she projected her true nature.

Humor was certainly not left behind in some of her disclaimers in the titles of wickedness bestowed upon her. In "The Story of my Life," a series syndicated in early 1916, she began with these words: "In the beginning let me make it clear that I did not want to write this story. I would prefer that the shameful matters be kept locked in my own bosom. But the public has clamored so long and loudly for my private affairs, secrets, etc. that I feel it is due it that I bare my history." Having bared so much else, the history was undoubtedly due.

"I am not as black as I am painted," Theda continued. "I was born beautiful. There is some ominous fate that stalked in my path when I was but a young girl trying to get along. It clutched me by the throat, dragged me aloft into its murky clouds, stifled my good resolutions and put me in pictures at a salary of $1,500 a week. I sincerely hope no other girl shall be preyed upon in this fashion."

This is Theda in midstream, attempting to be like everyone else for a moment but swiftly reverting to the vampire invention. About the most distressing thing her ghost writer could dredge up for this supposedly revealing memoir was the fact that her school life was unhappy due to her great beauty: "I was not popular with the girls. They said they were afraid of me because my eyes were so big and black and strange-looking. There is no greater tragedy in life than that of a child who is not popular with her playmates. Night after night I'd wear myself out sobbing over it. . . ."

The approach really wasn't very convincing, so back to the vampire fantasy, with a barrage of figures invented by Fox publicity. Theda Bara, it was announced, had "deceived fifty men with her wiles, made one hundred families suffer, caused fifty children and one hundred fifty wives to beg her to give back to them their daddies and their husbands."

The reincarnation story and the Sphinx bit were also given more mileage. Notwithstanding her ambivalent desire to throw off the vampire image, Theda went along. "I can tell you of at least four times that I have been on earth, yes, and I believe I could relate to you convincing incidents of those lives," she told

Archie Bell. "I lived in ancient Egypt, probably at Thebes. That city is as vivid in my recollection as the streets of New York today. I remember crossing the Nile on barges to Karnak and Luxor as plainly as I recall crossing the Hudson on the ferry today to come to the studio at Fort Lee. I do not expect other people to believe this. I know they will not, so usually I avoid mentioning the subject because people will think either that I am seeking sensational and cheap publicity, or that I am a fool. And I am not a fool."

People thought many things about Theda Bara, but few thought her a fool, certainly not Archie Bell as he watched her reach into the low-necked bodice of her gown to pull out two clay models of the ancient Egyptian god, Amen-Ra. "He was my protector in the days of long ago, and he is my protector today," she declared. "When I was a little girl, my mother was walking me past a curio shop in Paris, where these were on view in the window. I wanted them because I recognized them in an instant. I went back each day and stood fascinated by them. One day my mother bought them for me, and they have never left me since. I sleep with them. They are always concealed about my clothing when I am acting."

For months in her meetings with reporters, when the maid brought in her vampire's lunch of raw beef and lettuce leaves, the statuettes of Amen-Ra reposed on either side of the plate.

Having made it clear that Theda believed in crystal balls and the stars, the next step was to elaborate on these superstitions. Theda was soon telling the press that she thought it was bad luck to meet a funeral—certainly there had been bad luck somewhere in the path of the deceased. She went on to tell of talismans and charms she believed in:

"I have an emerald ring given to me by a blind sheik, celebrated for his learning and wisdom. Cut into the emerald are a camel and a dog. The sheik told me the ring had come down to him for generations and was more than 2,000 years old. He gave it to me because he was the last of his family. He made me promise that should any male child be born to me, I was to hang the ring about the child's neck and teach him to pray for him and to read Arabic. The old sheik was more than 110. One of his ancestors lived, he said, to be 143. I was told that by keeping the ring, I would live long and that by praying to it I would get what I asked for. Have I tried? Yes, and I have always gotten what I prayed for.

"I also have a small crystal globe on which are engraved a bear and a bunch of dates. This, too, is a gift. I wear it suspended about my neck, waking and sleeping. It protects me from accidents. How do I know? Well, I never have had an accident.

"A maltese coral I keep to ward off attacks by animals—particularly dogs. All stones have the faculty of transmitting bad luck as well as good luck. A golden hand I wear to ward off the evil eye. I have had it since I was a child in Italy.

"A sailor gave me a shark's tooth to protect me from the dangers of the sea. My little golden Inca god was given me by a Mexican, who promised that it would always protect me against fire and flood.

"While I wear many talismans, I do not think I am more superstitious than a lot of other persons. There are a lot of other things I believe in, but it would take too long to tell all of them."

From this account, it appears that Theda was remarkably well fortified against various accidents, attacks from dogs, dangers of the sea—which one can only hope included sharks, said to have been after her well-fleshed body—as well as fire and flood. Even long life, of which she had earlier despaired, appeared to be assured if she prayed hard enough for it while wearing the 110-year-old sheik's 2,000-year-old ring. To the paraphernalia that she said she wore constantly on her person, she had added the small crystal globe engraved with a bear and a bunch of grapes. In none of the scenes from her films did the clay statuettes of Amen-Ra or the crystal ball become visible to the naked eyes, however, although the body of the Vampire was discernible from every angle, in costumes scarcely able to conceal a blush.

If the various talismans brought Theda everything she asked

for, they no doubt helped her to obtain several sympathetic roles early in the new year, 1916. Not, however, before the execution of two more unrelenting vampire characterizations. In *Gold and the Woman* she played Juliet de Cordova, a Mexican adventuress, who did in one Colonel Dent because the colonel had fleeced some Indians out of their valuable land. In *The Eternal Sappho*, loosely based on Alphonse Daudet's original, Theda wrecked the lives of four men long before the end of the fifth reel. She did so in a series of stunning and daring new gowns, apparently enjoying each moment, if the violent heavings of her bosom were any indication.

Capacity crowds greeted these latest efforts, but once again the hard-working star had had enough. In theaters across America, D. W. Griffith's great epic, *The Birth of a Nation*, was giving films a new dimension, and Theda Bara wanted to broaden her own artistic scope. The studio offered her the role of Cigarette, the pure, untainted heroine of romantic novelist Ouida's *Under Two Flags*. As the impulsive, warmhearted Cigarette, a good horsewoman, the favorite of the foreign legion, Cigarette plays out her life on the sands of the African desert. With this provocation, the Fox publicity machine shifted into high gear.

Recalling Theda's birth just a camel's throw from the Sphinx, it was brought to light that as a child she would often jump on the back of one of the Arabian horses in her father's camp and ride out across the waste for miles. The Bedouins of the desert came to know the little girl and looked for her in the mornings, it was said. Often she would stop and eat dates and drink camel's milk with them. Then she would leap on her horse and be off across the sands before they knew it.

Shooting on location in the Florida dunes, Theda suddenly recalled childhood experiences that previous films had not drawn forth. "It was just like getting home again," she told the press. "I could feel the dryness of the desert air in my throat and the playing of desert sands about my bare feet. It's a strange coincidence. I was born at an oasis in the Sahara, and now in the Ouida story I am back again. There seems to be a strange fate which haunts my work in the picture and draws me back often to the scenes where I spent my childhood or my earlier years."

One of the studio's big efforts in the new film was a raging sandstorm, which director J. Gordon Edwards created by having several carloads of grain and chaff propelled by giant fans. Theda avowed that for her it was an old experience. "One of my earliest recollections is linked with a simoon which swept across the desert and scattered destruction in its path," she related. "A heated, beating sand went before it and almost buried our tent. We crept close within it and afterward had to dig our way through to the air. It was almost stifling, and I remember how I cried as my mother and father lay close against the ground, pushing their way through the treacherous sand."

Summing it all up, Theda said: "Acting in this picture has aroused the call of the desert in me again, and I sometimes feel as if I'd like to return there and live again, for a short time, the wild, unruly life of the desert children."

"In her wildness, her quick fun, and tenderness, and flashing anger, she gives a good impersonation of an untrammeled, untutored girl," wrote the *Chicago Tribune* of Theda's performance. The *New Orleans States* was similarly effusive: "Especially good is she in that thrilling climax, where, riding in the teeth of a desert sandstorm, she hurried to her beloved Bertie with papers saving his life from the firing squad, only to reach his side at the command, "Fire!" and receive in her bosom the bullets intended for him."

After *Under Two Flags* Theda incarnated the tragic Isabell in the classic tearjerker *East Lynne.* The "good" Theda continued her binge in *Her Double Life,* in which she dropped her vampire role for a nurse's kit. At this time artist Jose Ruchti painted her as the Guardian Angel of Paradise and declared: "Her eyes, her form, her mannerisms, her very soul, suggest the seraphic."

Einar Linden composed a song about Theda, which was published under the title, "Those Perilous Eyes," but William Fox's star went straight into another sympathetic role, that of Juliet in a film version of Shakespeare's classic of thwarted love. As its contribution to the Bard's tercentenary, Metro Pictures was also filming *Romeo and Juliet,* featuring one of the screen's most popular couples, Francis X. Bushman and Beverly Bayne. The $300,000 Fox version had handsome Harry Hillard playing Romeo.

"I have never found any part which called for the keen psychological insight and detailed analysis that was necessary for interpreting the character of Juliet," Theda reported to the press. In her delineation of the role she found it appropriate to give Juliet a touch and a twinge of the vampire, and the result was highly acclaimed. The critic for *Photoplay,* the leading fan magazine, found that "histrionically, Miss Bara is a better Juliet than Miss Bayne, for she brings to the play's tragic moments all the steam-heat that the cool Beverly lacks." A few uncharitable viewers felt that Theda was a bit sophisticated for the role of the 14-year-old Capulet, but even these carpers admired the "usual intensity" of her overall portrayal.

The sympathetic characterizations had found an audience, but it was not as large as the studio had hoped. When the public clamored for Theda Bara to return to her vampire roles, William Fox declared: "The public be pleased." The titles of his star's next pictures were self-explanatory: *Fires of Hate, The Vixen,* and *The Tiger Woman.*

"It would be difficult to locate a more despicable type of femininity," wrote one critic of the woman who trampled over her own sister in *The Vixen.* "It is true that I have no heart," the vixen says at one point, "but then I am more comfortable without one." "The havoc wrought by Theda as a vamp is second only to the European armies," wrote *Variety* of *The Tiger Woman.* "If the Germans are in need of quick aid, as reported, they might call on Theda Bara to bust up the armies of the Allies."

"In this play Theda Bara kills more men than William Hart in his most desperate moments, and the wholesale damage that strews her pathway would put a Kansas cyclone to shame," exclaimed the *New York Mirror.* Truly, an enterprising undertaker could have built a booming business simply by camping on her screen trail.

As 1916 ended, Theda ground out her tenth picture of the year, playing a gypsy dancing girl in *Darling of Paris*. Apart from the fact that she was surrounded by goats and gargoyles, the story bore only a very remote resemblance to Victor Hugo's *Notre Dame de Paris (Hunchback of Notre Dame)*, on an episode of which it was ostensibly based.

For her public Theda Bara issued a New Year's statement, which outlined her hopes for the future: "To go on with my art, inculcating into the minds of that great, big-hearted, at the same time supercritical public, the fact that I am only portraying imaginary characters—that they think of me not in terms of Vampire, but as a woman who is giving her very being to the screen, for the amusement of the public. . . ."

The year 1917 was to bring prosperity for Theda. By the terms of a new contract with Fox, her weekly salary was to increase at the rate of $50 per picture. Since she made close to one picture a month, this added up to a total year-end increase of $600 a week. The contract also contained certain remarkable stipulations, which decreed for Theda the life of a cloistered nun. Key prohibitions were the following:

(1) Theda was not to marry during the contract period, three years.

(2) She was not to go shopping unless heavily veiled.

(3) She was not to go to her costumer unless her features were entirely covered.

(4) She was not to take her daily constitutional in the light of day, but only at night and then heavily veiled.

(5) She was not to ride in public conveyances such as street cars, subways, or elevated trains.

(6) She was to ride in her limousine only on condition that the windows were curtained with net, through which she could see but not be seen. Needless to say, a relative in Egypt was providing the gauze for the curtains.

(7) She was not to attend public Turkish baths—of which she was very fond—but would have a private Turkish bath built in her home.

The private Theda was reduced by this contract to an isolation that makes Greta Garbo seem like a screaming magpie. The
screen Theda continued to be almost omnipresent, and Egypt
was about to be her stomping ground in a $500,000 film life of
Cleopatra. On the desert, adjoining bean fields, in California's
Ventura County, Fox technicians erected copies of the Pyramids and the Sphinx. On a pseudo Nile almost within the cor-
porate limits of Los Angeles they recreated the waterfront of
Alexandria, while forty miles away, on the beach at Balboa, a
fleet of warcraft was assembled for the desperate sea battle,
which was to be a highlight of the film. Roman palaces, the
Forum, the royal barge all were springing into being for an epic
that was to be populated by "a cast of thousands," among them
15,000 extras and more than 2,000 horses.

Ensconced for the first time on the West Coast, Theda Bara
made several references to the "effete East" and gave her view
of the colorful empress who died at the age of 39. "I believe
that Cleopatra was little different from the usual girl of today,"
she said. "I believe that the story of her tragic life, if placed in a
modern setting, with its heroine a girl of the working classes,
would be found almost commonplace. There would be little to
distinguish it from the cases of a thousand girls of our own
day."

If Theda was going to opt for a simple Cleo with whom every
shopgirl could identify, William Fox decidedly favored an
exotic Theda, upon whom all could gaze in wonder. "The
coming of Theda Bara was prophesied by the ancient Egyp-
tians!" read the headlines of a press story, the elaboration of
which was truly remarkable. It stated that the inner walls of a
recently opened tomb had disclosed hieroglyphics that
emanated from the Egyptian god of evil. Although badly worn
by the centuries, these ancient writings were legible enough for
scientists to decipher an amazing forecast. It read as follows:

> I, Rhames, priest of Set, tell you this: She shall seem a snake to most
> men; she shall lead them to sin, and to their destruction. Yet she shall
> not be so. She shall be good and virtuous, and kind of heart; but she

shall not seem so to most men. For she shall not be that which she appears! She shall be called . . .

The Greek letter *theta* finished the inscription, and, according to the Fox archaeologists, its insertion was not without purpose. It was evidently the writer's intent to name the woman about whom he was prophesying, and by Grimm's law the d and t were interchangeable in many languages. Making this slight emendation in the Greek letter, one got the correct name of the famous screen vampire: Theda Bara. The story concluded with word that the wondrous tablets had been moved from the tomb near Thebes, where they had been found, and were now on exhibition in the Boulak Museum in Cairo.

Gradually, further discoveries were announced. Theda Bara, it was stated, had in an earlier life been the original daughter of Seti, high priest of the Pharaohs. The immortal remains of her maternal ancestor Umslopagaas had recently been unsandwiched from her sarcophagus in the pyramid of Chephren, where they had lain for more than three thousand years. They had been put on public view.

The studio publicity machine received a slight setback after it announced that key emotional scenes in *Cleopatra* would be played against an old Egyptian chant dug up with some mummified remains and carried down through the ages by Cleo's posterity. Investigation by a musical sleuth showed the tune in question to be a modern dance by one Gabriel-Marie. It was moreover called "La Cinquantaine," or "The Golden Wedding Anniversary."

As filming progressed, the unruffled studio said that its star had received a beautifully illumined card bearing strange cabalistic signs. Since Miss Bara had made a study of Egyptian lore, she herself had deciphered the card's message, which translated as follows: "Homage to the beautiful lady Theda Bara, sacred woman chosen for the service of the Gods. O protect Thou her body against all things evil."

In a letter accompanying the "ancient blessing," the unknown sender said that he had made a lifelong study of ancient Egypt and that he was the reincarnation of one of the courtiers who attended Queen Cleopatra. He added that his research in and around the pyramids and with old papyrus rolls convinced him that Theda was actually the twentieth-century reincarnation of the renowned Egyptian queen.

"I felt the blood of the Ptolemys coursing through my veins," Theda said after completing the picture. "I know that I actually am a reincarnation of Cleopatra. It is not a mere theory in my mind. I have positive knowledge that such is the case. I live Cleopatra, I breathe Cleopatra, I *am* Cleopatra!"

The elaborate build-up paid off for the studio. With Fritz Leiber as Julius Caesar and Thurston Hall as Mark Antony, *Cleopatra* played at special prices, with a $1 maximum. An estimated five million people flocked to showings within a year. "An uncommonly fine picture," wrote the *New York Times*. "Miss Bara contributes a thoroughly successful portrait of the Serpent of the Nile. It is the finest sort of film fare . . . and fans are certain to flock to it." The *New York Tribune*, "completely overwhelmed," said the spectacle "simply beggars description, and Theda Bara has never before looked so regally beautiful."

Although many critics felt that Theda had never been better than as the imperious Egyptian temptress, the rare dissenters included the *Brooklyn Eagle*, which liked everything in the film save the star. "She makes a burlesque of the Serpent of the Nile and is never for one moment convincing," said the *Eagle*'s critic. "She could never tempt a man to be late for dinner, much less to give up the throne of Rome. When she was not repulsive, she was funny."

It is worth noting that the *Eagle* had long waged a campaign against Theda Bara, deploring her theatrical trickery, facial gymnastics, and bodily contortions, calling her a second-rate actress who would never play any sort of roles except those that gave her a chance to throw an emotional fit in the key scenes. "She gives the spectators their money's worth in exactly the same fashion that a prizefighter delights the devotés of the ring when he pounds an opponent into a pulp," said one of the paper's indictments. "Theda Bara pounds emotion until there isn't anything left of it. In most of her work she is a maudlin emotionalist who daubs the colors on her palette with a shoebrush. There is nothing easier for an experienced actress than the vampire type of character. It is hysterical acting raised to the nth power; it is sheer emotionalism gone mad; it is, in fact, everything except great art. Simplicity, intelligence, and restraint are the three qualities that go into the making of any lasting success on the legitimate stage. She has none of the three."

To some degree Theda might have agreed. "My own idea of a vampire is the thoroughly human woman who is a blend of good and bad impulses. The absolutely heartless, cold vampire of fiction is false and artificial," she said on one occasion. Again and again she begged and cajoled her studio into giving her worthier screenplays. As a result of her pleadings a curious lineup of stories came her way, hokeyed up classics alternating with maudlin melodramas, both giving way again and again to no-holds-barred, stereotyped vampire plots that the public—and many critics—demanded.

During 1917 she filmed *Camille* and *Madame DuBarry*, along with *Her Greatest Love*, the last based on Ouida's melodramatic novel *Moths*. "Had I a heart less kind," wrote Louella Parsons, "I could fill many pages telling why Miss Bara should never be cast as a young girl, unsophisticated and innocent." Louella's analysis of the end product was, "A decidedly trashy moving picture." Like many others she did not like Theda minus horns and cloven hoofs.

Heart and Soul, based on Rider Haggard's *Jess*, was Theda's next vehicle. "It's a noble character, all right, but any plain girl can play that kind of a part," the *Los Angeles Examiner* said of her effort. "Why take a raving beauty like Miss Bara and smother her physical charms with demurely parted hair and sports clothes? Personally I like her better with fascinating negligees swirling about her, heavily tinted fingernails, and a cigarette between her lips."

The Rose of Blood filled the *Examiner*'s bill, so much so that Chicago's film censor, Major Funkhouser, became upset and wired the Department of Justice in Washington, D.C., requesting assistance in preventing the film from being shown. The department turned the telegram over to the Committee on Public Information. The committee in turn asked Fox to send a print of the production, which depicted the efforts of revolutionaries to overthrow the Czar of Russia. Representatives of the War Department were among those invited to a special showing. When they found the film neither a threat to morality nor to the war effort, *The Rose of Blood* was released for exhibition in Chicago without cuts or changes.

Vampire films were far removed from the concerns of World War I. To some degree they were no doubt a form of escape from that harsh reality. However, with America's entry into the conflict in April, 1917, Theda Bara became one of the country's most effective saleswomen of Liberty Bonds, selling more than $300,000 worth on a memorable afternoon in New York's Bryant Park. The 158th Infantry Regiment, composed mostly of Arizonans stationed at California's Camp Kearney, named her their godmother. Theda went to visit her troops. When on her arrival they stood at present arms, she burst into tears and told them it was the most glorious day of her life.

Theda's friends at Fox felt that the patriotic angle could be profitably exploited. They concocted a dream, during which Theda had allegedly seen the war come to an end through the instrumentality of a woman. Each aspect of the dream was minutely described and relayed by papers no less respected than the *New York Times.* Only the *Cleveland Plain Dealer* looked askance at the story. "If you or I ventured to state we had a vision in which we saw peace in the world war restored by a woman, we would be looked upon with tolerant commiseration by our friends, and perhaps clapped into the nearest nutty shanty by our enemies," wrote the Ohio journal. "But when the vision is Theda Bara's, it makes a 600-word story calculated to make the superstitious and ignorant believe in Theda's occult powers."

The Fox minions picked up this criticism and turned it back upon itself. Theda Bara was greatly affected by the sufferings of the French, they declared, so much so that at times she appeared to lose her personality and to be under the sway of inexplicable influences.

The filming of a French classic, *Camille*, began to look almost like a patriotic gesture when seen in the emotional haze created by the studio; and Theda's ensuing portrayal of the title role in *Madame Dubarry* gave Fox a golden opportunity to recall her Bourbon nose and Gallic ancestry.

The renowned Vampire herself contributed the screenplay for *The Soul of Buddha*, inspiration for which came to her when she read that Mata Hari, the East Indian dancer, had been executed as a German spy. This first attempt as a screen author was completed in the time it took Theda to cross the continent on a train—close to five days. The film provoked the *Chicago Tribune* reviewer, Mae Tinee (along with the *Brooklyn Eagle*, the *Tribune* never succumbed to the Vampire's charms), into a savage critique:

"Funny little Theda's back again with her bag of tricks in a funny picture built around a scenario she wrote herself," said Tinee. "As in all Bara pictures, the picture is all Bara—Bara making faces, Bara ogling, Bara wriggling. Bara shoulders—and everything. As a Javanese dancer, consecrated to Buddhism by her mother, she minces and flaunts through the temple exercises. During some incantation or other to which spectators are allowed, she casts the fatal look upon one Sir John Dare, a major in that portion of the English army stationed there. Instantly it's all off with Sir John. He meets her in the sacred grove that night, carries her away, and marries her, thereby bringing down on her head the wrath of the Buddhists and on his own—disgrace—for his resignation is demanded by his Colonel. The rest of the picture is a sodden conglomeration entirely uninteresting and unoriginal, with Miss Bara finally dying an air-clawing death at the hands of the high priest who has tracked her over two continents, unobserved despite the fact that he wears a turkish towel wrapped about his head and rolls the whites of his eyes in broad daylight. And, he stalks.

Ah, well—!" Thus Theda played into the hands of her enemies with a routine vampire of her own creation.

In 1918 and 1919 Theda Bara made *Under the Yoke,* a pulsating drama of the Philippines, and *The Forbidden Path.* She made *When a Woman Sins,* which Mae Tinee called "as punk as most of the photoplays in which I have been so unfortunate as to witness Miss Bara"; and she made *The She Devil, The Light, The Message of the Lilies, La Belle Russe, Siren's Song, When Men Desire,* and *A Woman There Was.*

She also made a much-ballyhooed version of *Salome* with a beardless John the Baptist. When a St. Louis reviewing committee said that the film made too seductive an appeal to the senses and found Theda "overbold and underclad," the beleaguered star had one of the last explosions of her dazzling but relatively brief career. "I challenge each and every one of these statements," she declared. "Hypocrisy is to blame for the present-day point which makes it 'sinful' for a woman to expose parts of her body on stage or screen, although it is conventional for her to do it at a bathing beach. Evil to him who evil thinks. I never think of the flesh when I am working in a role such as Salome. I concentrate upon the character and its interpretation, and if proper interpretation of the story calls for a scantily clad creature, the latter is only an incident."

"As Salome, Miss Bara does not resemble the tigerish princess of Judea as much as a neurasthenic taking sun-baths," an unkind critic wrote of her interpretation. "No wonder Herod killed Salome after her dance."

The continued assault on her "art" and the condemnation of Vampire roles kept Theda searching for alternatives, but with little success. "Whenever I try to be a nice, good little thing, you all stay away from my pictures," she chided her fans. Nevertheless, in mid-1919 she persuaded Fox to cast her as the sweet little colleen of rhyme and story in *Kathleen Mavourneen.* Torn cotton dresses replaced the shimmering gowns of the vampire, and golden Mary Pickford curls framed the famous Bara eyes. "This is the best role I've ever had," Theda glowed. "There isn't the slightest trace of the Vampire in *Kathleen.*

More than ever before, her fans stayed away in droves. This time the unhappy star remained adamant. "The word 'Vampire' has become a stench in my cinematographic nostrils," she told Fox, and again she demanded that the studio give her better and more varied roles, spending more on the pictures and upping her own salary. Her three-year contract had run out, and her bargaining position was not as strong as she had anticipated. Earlier in the year when she demanded a raise from $1,500 per week to $4,000, Fox had acquiesced. Now she wanted the ante raised to $5,000 per week. (This was small pickings compared to Mary Pickford's $1 million a year.)

Despite a general slump in the film industry, it is possible that Fox would have met Theda's figure had she not made other demands. "I will never again pursue one line of work to the exclusion of all others," she insisted. "A one-track mind is bound to go to seed. A one-way art is sure to grow threadbare. I want to portray characters true to life whatever they may be. Really, there are very few vampires in everyday life. The vampire woman of the screen is absurdly exaggerated. Sometimes she comes very close to being ridiculous instead of dangerous. Carmen was not a vamp, though the public so insisted when I was the lady of the stiletto. Why they even tried to make a vamp out of poor sweet little Juliet just because I was behind her. Imaging Juliet vamping."

Theda described the sort of life that went with her screen vamping. "Five practically uninterrupted years of vamping have drawn my nerves pretty taut," she said. "I have seldom had longer than a week between pictures, and even this was not my own. It was replete with dressmakers and costumers and period experts, days of intensive preparation for work to come. And gradually those vampire emotions began to weigh me down. I felt heavy, depressed. There were not enough laughs in my life, and I do so love to laugh."

Even the amusing incidents didn't register. Theda recalled a letter from an Oriental admirer, which read: "Please pardon for addressing honorable self, but will so kind send honorable portrait of honorable self as honorably naked as possible."

"How is any girl going to inspire such requests and keep sane?" Theda asked. "How is she going to wake up with a dozen or more similar missives on her desk and keep her reason? It can't be done, and so far as I am concerned, it is not going to be done. I will not slink and writhe and wriggle day in and day out. I demand to bob my curls and climb trees and love for love's own sake. I want to be—well, natural."

No one wanted Theda Bara to be natural. Fox refused to renew her contract. No other firm offer came her way. Rumor had it that she was going to form her own company, that she was dickering with Paramount, that she was talking to foreign filmmakers. Whatever was about to happen, Theda let it be known that she would have to be exploited as a symbol of purity; her purpose to spread happiness. Reluctantly she vamped once more to fill out her contract for Fox in *Lure of Ambition*, released in November 1919. And then she vamped no more for the screen. The film career of one of Hollywood's most magnetic stars ended with the same dramatic speed with which it had begun, though at the time no one was aware of its being over.

Years later MGM was to proclaim "Garbo Talks," but in early 1920 the big entertainment news was "The Sphinx Will Speak." Noted entrepreneur A.H. Woods signed the screen's leading vampire for a new play entitled *The Blue Flame*; rehearsals were to begin almost immediately in New York.

Theda Bara's earliest ambition had been to perform for the theater. When screen fame came her way, it did not erase that ambition from her mind. "First I must make all the world realize that I am an actress in pictures," she said early in her career, "and then I shall stand before them, and they must feel what they have never felt from looking at my pictures. I will thrill them. I promise you that. Give me the play, one that shows real life, and I will give you something to think about."

The Blue Flame hardly showed "real life," but it certainly gave Theda's following something to think about. The four-act melodrama by George V. Hobart and John Willard was based on an earlier effort by Leta Vance Nicholson. Producer Woods bought complete rights from the three writers for $35,000. The

money having been paid, the authors' passion for art appeared
to evaporate. Not one even attended rehearsals. In view of what
they had wrought, this may have been prudent.

The Blue Flame is the story of a young agnostic named John
Varnum (Alan Dinehart) who has carried scientific research to
the point at which he can work miracles by means of an electric
"resurrection ray." Varnum denies God because he himself has
discovered the secret of death and the mystery of creating life
through this ray. His persistent irreligiosity brings keen distress
to his fianceé, the soulful Ruth Gordon (Theda Bara), ardent in
settlement work and an intensely Orthodox believer.

The first act, uneventful, establishes Ruth as the pure, gentle
heroine. In the second the action picks up. There is a
thunderstorm on stage. Ruth is killed by lightning in Varnum's
laboratory. Through Varnum's efforts she slowly regains life
and consciousness, but in the process a tiny blue flame is discovered flitting from her body. The scientist has restored his
sweetheart's life—without a soul! The new Ruth has the eyes of
a tiger and the tongue of a serpent; her blood is the icy stream
that flows from an Arctic glacier. She is, in fact, the old Theda
Bara, the vampire. She exerts an evil influence on all with whom
she comes in contact. She is a woman without morals:
cold-blooded, worldly, following only her craving for pleasure.

The recharged Ruth induces Varnum to marry her. Soon he
feels her long arms twining about his neck and hears her shout
that ringing challenge of the vampiric sisterhood, "Kiss me,
dearie!" When he is unable to supply her extravagant demands
for luxury, she practices her wiles on other men, going on a
rampage that tramples all underfoot—her husband, his best
friend, a young girl, a burglar, a stricken mother, and even a
merchant in Chinatown. "To be good is only to be forgotten,"
she shouts defiantly, vowing that she is going to be "bad enough
to be remembered for the ages."

The final act reveals the wholesale slaughter to be a bad
dream. Varnum awakens to find his heroine as sweet as ever.
Moreover, having seen the sordid fate of a disbeliever, he is now
ready to change his agnostic ways for a path more spiritual.

"I have withdrawn temporarily from the screen to play for

A.H. Woods in this remarkable drama," Theda Bara told reporters before her out-of-town opening in Boston in March, 1920. "Many people have been asking me in what plays I appeared before. I may say that it doesn't matter. I have been on the stage here and in England, but I believe that the artist's present is all that counts. . . . As to who I am and where I came from, I am Theda Bara, a resident of the United States, an actress by profession, circumstance, and inclination. That is all one needs to know about me to enjoy the play."

Theda had certainly not forgotten her publicity cues. In the out-of-town engagements her screen fans flocked to see her, with police holding crowds in check in Boston, Pittsburgh, and Washington. Working under a weekly guarantee of $1,500 plus 50 percent of the profits, she received a total of $7,500 for the final sold-out week in Boston.

On March 15 *The Blue Flame* opened at the Shubert Theater in New York, to tremendous fanfare. Thousands were turned away at the box office. Among the first-night audience were such celebrities of the period as Norma Talmadge, producer Lewis Selznick, Florence Reed, director Robert Leonard, and Mae Murray. They attended the unfolding of the play with hilarious incredulity, but they were kind and respectful toward the star.

Not so with the critics. They proceeded to unleash on the shapely head of Theda Bara excited abuse the likes of which had not been seen or heard since the days when the woebegone Cherry Sisters performed behind protective chicken-wire netting on the Bowery.

In Heywood Broun, Theda found her most severe antagonist. He described her in these terms: "Ruth Gordon, the heroine of the play, used cocaine, spoke crossly to her maid, instigated the theft of an emerald, murdered a young man, took money from a gentleman other than her husband, said 'Go to hell!,' lied to a burglar, broke a young girl's heart, refused to see a stricken mother, visited a Chinese merchant after midnight, gave her latchkey to a rounder, and smoked a cigarette. Ruth was bad. Miss Bara kept within the city ordinances, but she was not so

very good either. At the end of the third act she made a speech
in which she said that God had been very kind to her. Probably
she referred to the fact that at no time during the course of the
evening did the earth open and swallow up the authors, the star,
and all the company."

"Silence is golden," said the *New York World.* "When we
watch pictures, we seldom worry about the quality of voice that
their heroes and heroines possess. . . . There at the Shubert
Theater we beheld the picture come to life, and we were
inclined to admit that life was something of a detriment. The
picture spoke—and we laughed. The picture took into her live
arms several men and squeezed them into kisses—and we
tittered. Her vampire speeches were uttered with matter-of-fact
and colorless rigidity. She had a schoolgirl's recitatif, a western
monotony, and a sort of black alpaca dreariness."

The schoolgirl motif was repeated by half a dozen other
reviewers, including Alexander Woollcott, who said, "She
speaks her lines distinctly and rather like a young girl at a high
school commencement exercise—with an additional touch of
elegance achieved by the simple process of pronouncing
pocketbook as if it were 'pawkitbook'. . . . And she displays a
fine self-possession which enabled her to proceed last evening
with unflinching gravity when the audience lost control of itself
and shook with laughter."

While Woollcott felt that Theda Bara had a pleasant enough
voice, other critics, such as Louis DeFoe, found it thin and
"meaningless." Said DeFoe: "It shows what very slight attain-
ments are needed for a successful career as a movie actress. With
sufficient self-assurance it is plain that anyone can become a
queen of the screens."

More charitable commentators felt that Theda had battled
nobly against lines like "I've got to have $85,000 in a hurry,"
and "I'll shake you like I shake my shimmy." *Variety* provided
a balanced roundup: "There tripped on the stage a slender,
girlish person in an adorable chiffon frock, a young woman with
a chin delicately modeled, a baby doll of a face, slender fingers,
hands and wrists, and a voice that, while it was to an extent still

self-conscious and a bit affected, had nevertheless pleasant, even notes in it. She no more came on than the applause started—for this was Theda Bara. For two minutes, perhaps, she bowed and bowed and bowed. . . . Presently the audience paused, and the show went on. Miss Bara showed careful training. She has not yet learned how to get around the stage, to sit down and get up, but otherwise, she was satisfactory enough."

The inability to sit down and get up and to move around the stage were perhaps greater handicaps than *Variety* anticipated. Or Theda Bara. "I really don't know what the critics said about me. I haven't read them at all. They might disturb me," she said. "I do not play to Broadway. Broadway is the workshop of theatrical people. I play to the ordinary people who go to the theaters or the movies to be entertained, not to compete."

Despite bad reviews, *The Blue Flame* sold out in its first weeks, clearly a managerial coup for A.H. Woods. Huge crowds, mostly women, milled about Shubert Alley at theater time, hoping to catch a glimpse of the star or to examine her motor car, painted yellow, the doors embellished with figures meant to be Egyptian but sometimes mistaken for Hebrew. By April, however, *Variety* reported that the show was selling seats at cut-rate prices. Producer Woods wisely put *The Blue Flame* back on the road, playing Providence, Rhode Island, and other eastern cities to full houses.

"This is only the beginning. I am going to appear in other plays, for I'm anxious to do big things," Theda announced. One of her vampire rivals, actress Olga Petrova, interviewed her and wrote cuttingly, "I was tempted to suggest laundering elephants."

In June, 1920, Theda Bara accompanied her sister Lori to Paris on a shopping expedition. Lori met a newspaperman, fell in love, and married. Theda returned unostentatiously to America and resumed her role in *The Blue Flame*. During the Chicago run she met William Fox on Randolph Street, but the two did not speak. It was said that Theda was more convinced than ever that Fox had driven her out of pictures by assigning impossible scenarios to her. At the end of the year the touring star ended her contract with Woods amid rumors that she was to become the bride of theatrical manager Tom Bodkin.

Although Bodkin never entered her life, other rumors of marriage bore fruit in June, 1921. Theda married Charles Brabin, an Englishman who had directed her last two pictures, *Kathleen Mavourneen* and *Lure of Ambition*. Brabin, forty-one, had been married before. For Theda it was the first and only marriage of her life. With the Vampire no longer under contract to Fox, that studio paid scant attention to the event. Only a terse press release was sent out when the couple returned from a three-week honeymoon, spent in the wilds of Nova Scotia on the Bay of Fundy.

"I would tell every girl . . . that the glamour of a career fades beside that of a happy marriage," Theda said near the end of the year. "That is the most supreme happiness given us mortals. I was a long time finding mine, but I did, you know."

Although in any meaningful sense the career of one of the most talked-about actresses in the world was over, Theda was not yet aware of this. "I shall go back to the stage after a few pictures, but not in the same sort of horrid role I had in *The Blue Flame,*" she stated. Again the rumor mills started grinding, telling of plans to launch her own company and of a cross-country tour. The tour actually materialized. For twelve weeks in 1921 she made public appearances, on one occasion sharing the stage with evangelist Billy Sunday and drawing forth a response that dwarfed his. In the brief speech she made to each audience Theda told the women that she had not come to steal their husbands and that her vampire roles had strengthened the ideals of a good home by showing their contrast. Each talk concluded with a question and answer period.

"Will you all wish me to play the Vampire again?" she would ask, and the crowd would shout its approval.

"Would you also like to see me in the role of a good girl?" was her next question. In response there would be desultory and scattered handclapping. "Well, there you are," the crestfallen Theda would say. "It just looks as though you will not let me play anything but vampire parts. So I suppose I shall have to continue in parts somewhat similar to those I have played in the past."

Even a vampire role was to be denied to the star who had created the genre. In July, 1922, Lewis Selznick finally signed Theda Bara to a one-picture contract, but after a year of searching for a suitable scenario, the effort was abandoned.

One clue to that decision may well have come from Theda's old mentor, William Fox. When Fox remade *A Fool There Was* with a new star, a dark-eyed beauty named Estelle Taylor, the film's receipts at various houses were too small to pay electric bills for the mechanical piano. The simple fact of the matter was that Vampire roles no longer had box-office appeal. Where five or six years earlier each studio carried a vamp on its roster, and fans of every description gathered eagerly to watch them perform, it was now difficult to drag even a truant high school girl to see worldly women ruin men. Along with Theda, other popular practitioners, such as Valeska Suratt and Louise Blaum, were thus put out to pasture.

"I am not unaware of the general belief, especially among motion picture people, that the Vampire as we have always known her has been plentifully done," Theda said. "It is time she applied her arts for some more worthy purpose than simply to take away some other woman's husband or sweetheart. So on my return to the screen I am going to be a new kind of Vampire. I am going to be a Vampire who does some good in the world. I am going to be a Vampire who motivates."

When the former star finally returned to the screen, in 1925, it was as a warmed-over vamp in *The Unchastened Woman*, and in a series of comedies for Hal Roach. Bearing titles like *Madame Mystery*, the undistinguished efforts spoofed her own films. On this pathetic note she retired from the screen, never to appear again.

By that time the once brilliantly successful screen actress was herself aware that her era had passed. What had it all meant to Theda Bara? Money. International fame of the highest magnitude. But what else? Even before her film career sputtered its last quiet gasp, she had begun to look back, often in anger. In June, 1919, in a journal called *The Forum* she described herself as a charlatan, "a register of human emotions," and the moving picture art as "chiefly an art of lies." "There is something in the click of the camera as it registers the emotions, foot by foot, that demoralizes artistic expression," she wrote. "One becomes a species of human mechanism, speeding up all the deep sources of feeling, chopping them in bits to fit the inexorable ribbon of reel. It is an art of lies because it is limited to primitive impulses, to barren emotions; because it is a record of the feverish pulse of life, instead of the normal pulse. Everything must be told quickly, briefly, without a fair chance to develop artistic wants. These are confessions of intimate disappointment in the work that I have never overcome."

For Theda the ideal had always been the stage, and on that stage her idol was not the passionate Sarah Bernhardt but Eleanor Duse, whose "bloodless cheek of chaste renunciation" she so admired. Naturally the exaggerated Vampire roles distressed her. "I have been a vampire of fiction, not fact," she stated.

From the first, the atmosphere of the movie-drama had repelled Theda Bara. "The work was a constant jarring of sensibilities that would not down," she wrote. "What is any movie studio but a chamber of torture to the girl whose imagination is tainted with the flavor of artistic ideals? I am one of those women who like a great poem better than a poor one; Browning is more comforting to me than the philosophy of George M. Cohan. . . . With the success of *A Fool There Was* I renounced all former expectations of the art of acting. I cut my soul in two. One-half I kept for myself; the other half I gave to movies."

The half that Theda gave to the movies was a generous half. Each role was carefully researched. Libraries and authorities were consulted. For her very first part, in *A Fool There Was*, the great classical dancer Isadora Duncan instructed Theda in the lithe, sensual movements of the vampire. For *Salome*, Theda tried to absorb "the poetic impulse of Oscar Wilde." For

Cleopatra she spent weeks in the Egyptian wing of New York's Metropolitan Museum of Art and studied with its curator. If the studio was sometimes relaxed about historical detail, its star was not, and Theda designed many of her own clothes to give expression to her knowledge of an era.

In the matter of the characterization, which dominated her career, the star displayed certain clear and penetrating insights. "In playing this fascinating but despicable character the actress must make her ability to charm men seem plausible. She must not be merely flirtatious," she said of the vampire genre. "Her creation must manifest mental as well as physical charm. It must show traces of kleptomania. Every vampire in real life steals the affections of men partly because she cannot help stealing. The vampire is rarely the oversexed 'rag and bone and hank of hair' which Burne-Jones and Kipling painted and described. Far more likely is she to be the woman who gains amusement and a gratification of power-love out of conquering masculine hearts. It is sport for her. It entertains her, and in the end it becomes her occupation. She practices the art of it, studying how she can gain more skill, just as a yeggman schools his fingers in opening safes or just as a pickpocket trains himself in the business of the deft extraction of purses."

In many cases it was Theda's interpretation of a role that prevailed in the film. This was due to the fact that the man who made most of her films, director J. Gordon Edwards, felt that his function was strictly limited. "I believe that the less directing a director does, the better the picture will be—other things being equal," he once said. "Let the actress do a scene in her own way, let her have a chance with her temperament—that has always been my idea. Then you obtain grace, naturalness, the living thing, the thing that makes pictures as well as drama. I read the scenario once: then I throw it aside and never look at it again. A slavish following of its dictation would hamper me at every turn, making that which should be fluent and living into something static and dead."

"One time I asked my director about a certain scene," Theda herself related. "Do I repulse the advances of this man, or do I lead him on? 'Oh, just keep the audience guessing,' he said."

This type of direction naturally placed great responsibility and strain on the performer. Theda accepted the challenge and threw herself with astonishing energy into each role. "It is impossible to act without feeling," she said. "When I play a part, I live it. I am nobody else, and my companions often remind me that I say strange things and do strange things afterward, for I am still in the character. Sometimes I do not regain full self-possession until after I have slept."

Theda's intensity at times was awesome, and many of her comrades dreaded the ordeal of a violent screen tussle with her. For *Carmen* the director went to New York's Spanish colony to enlist the services of Fay Tunis, casting her as the cigarette girl with whom the star has a fight. So deeply did Theda become immersed in her role that she developed an actual violent dislike for the luckless girl. Day after day she watched her on the set with growing distaste. When the time came for their big scene, she pounced on the poor creature, clawed and struck and yanked at her long hair. When it was over Theda was covered with bruises—but the girl had fainted. She returned to her home in the Spanish Quarter and emoted no more for the treacherous cameras.

Similarly, the temperamental impulses of Cleopatra called for Theda to lay into an Italian actor who played Mark Antony's messenger. So powerful was her assault that the actor rushed off the set in fear of his life. "Just look at my back," he called to the director, who noted that real blood was running from real cuts and scratches inflicted by the aroused star. "Of course it was not strength at all, it was the emotional expression of Cleopatra's rage," Theda explained.

One can easily believe that vampiring on this scale would be exhausting. "After I played a few big scenes, I was like an invalid," Theda related. "I got into the automobile, went home as quickly as possible. My maid gave me a little warm milk or a light lunch, and I went to sleep and rested until far into the night. Then I felt like myself again and studied and read."

Work, study, reading: these were the steady diet of the

screen's wickedest wanton. If her contract demanded that she lead a life of seclusion, her nature had made it easy to enforce its provisions. Theda Bara had little taste for nightclubs and extravagant living. When she was not at the studio, she spent much of her time with her family in their Riverside Drive apartment. It held a plentiful supply of books and paintings but not a single leopard-skin rug.

"I'm the victim of overzealous press agents," Theda could say in 1920 as she began work in *The Blue Flame*. "This vampire stuff was started by a press agent named Goldfarp, when I made my first appearance, in *A Fool There Was*. He called me a 'Soulmate of the Devil' and started a pack of lies, which I'll never be able to live down. Why, he even said I was born two blocks from the Sphinx. You know I was never any nearer Egypt than an Egyptian cigarette, and I'll give you my word I was never anybody's soulmate. I was born in Cincinnati, and I have a perfectly good Jewish father. His name was Goodman. But I read so many lies about myself that I hardly know what is the truth anymore."

Theda confided at this time that she had had the option of reading press releases before they went out but that sometimes she did not get around to them until it was too late. "Anyway, some of them were so wild that we didn't think they would be printed, or that if they were printed, they wouldn't be believed," she said. "But they were printed, and they were believed, too, I suppose. The wildest press stories are the most successful ones. A lot of young ex-newspapermen wrote them. I think I kept a whole publicity staff working nights."

"And then the interviews," she went on. "They were staged. It took me hours to get ready for them. I had a special dress made that I never wore at other times. I remember one interview out in Chicago. My dress was black velvet and was made high at the throat. It was a terribly hot day, and all the windows were down. When the interview was over, I tore off that dress, and my sister and I sat down and roared with laughter about it."

As always, laughter was a saving grace, a necessary release, for

Theda Bara worked hard during her heyday, and she had few friends. It was perhaps a mature reflection that her years did not warrant, she once stated, but from early adolescence she sensed that she might meet only one or two human beings in life whom she would really like. Of the films she expected little in the way of close relationships. Nonetheless it was on the studio lot that she had met the man with whom she was to share her life.

Prior to her marriage, Hollywood's rumor mills found an almost complete lack of mileage in the romantic life of Theda Bara. In the few instances in which she was said to be on the verge of marriage, it seems that she had not even met the man in question. A passage from her 1919 article in *The Forum* is intriguing but too sketchy. Describing the years just preceding her screen debut, Theda says: "There followed a year or two of weird, incomprehensible experiences which are too intimate for the public eye. They concerned the usual emotional surprises that are the mystery of youth. They were perhaps romantic. They flourished for a time in that beautiful twilight called love."

One wonders if those "weird, incomprehensible experiences" were also painful for the fledgling actress, if perhaps they helped to foster that personal reserve that was in such stark contrast to her flamboyant screen personality. Apparently, Charles Brabin broke down whatever barriers were there by appealing to the qualities that Theda admired—intelligence, good manners, humor. She herself said he vamped her, but the manner was certainly conventional. He took her to lunch, engaged her in conversation she found stimulating, came to meet her mother. The six-foot-three Englishman threw in frequent dashes of Irish drollery, and gradually the courtship battle was won.

"I didn't want to be married. I hadn't ever cared about getting married," Theda said. But once the cautious bride had taken the final step, she remained married to Brabin for the 44 years that comprised the rest of her life. During that long period, no trace of scandal or scurrilous gossip touched the conservatively oriented woman, who on screen had been wantonness and wile incarnate.

Brabin continued prominent on the Hollywood scene, directing a steady stream of silent pictures and, later, a parallel skein of talkies under the banner of MGM. His wife spoke from time to time of breaking her retirement with a new film or a stage play, and her forthcoming autobiography was announced with some regularity. However, apart from a Beverly Hills Little Theater stage appearance in *Bella Donna*, in 1934—her reception in the melodrama was more polite than enthusiastic— nothing materialized. Theda Bara remained in retirement.

"She lives in Beverly Hills and doesn't do anything but have luncheons and dinners and that sort of thing," said her sister Lori. "Her retirement was on account of her husband, Charles Brabin, the famous director. He's English, you see. You know how they are?" Theda herself echoed this sentiment when asked about her absence from the screen. "The real reason why I left pictures, if you must know, is that I married an Englishman. Need I say more?"

Living in an unpretentious stucco house in Beverly Hills, with her husband, a Persian cat, and a maid, lorgnette-bearing Theda now occupied herself with society and good works, running committee meetings of charitable organizations. She became a leading figure in the exclusive Beverly Hills Women's Club. The 132 pounds that had filled out a voluptuous five-foot-six frame during her film career gradually increased under the impact of the superb cuisine for which she was noted. Dinner parties at the Brabins' drew the leading figures of the Hollywood movie colony, who knew they would also find cultivated conversation on the menu. Theda's contributions were delivered in a mild and pleasant British accent.

"If you were invited to her home, as I was the other day," wrote Adela Rogers St. Johns, "you would find a hostess who talks wittily, wisely, of music at the Hollywood Bowl, of new pictures acquired by the Museum, of European capitals and celebrities in every field who are her close friends."

Interviews with Theda Bara over the ensuing years were rare.

The reason, the former vampire candidly admitted, was that she was shy. She was also wary of having a photographer snap an unflattering photo. On one occasion, returning from a two-year European trip, she submitted to a reporter's questions and said, "I don't plan to do anything. I only live twenty-four hours a day, getting such happy fragments from life as I can. In this life we suffer so much, we try to find happiness when we can." Recently, she stated, she had seen some of her old pictures. They had "brought out the cold perspiration. It must have been the speed of the machines. They shot you through doors so fast you looked like a cannonball."

There were those who appeared annoyed by Theda Bara's comfortable retirement. Columnist Louis Sobol wrote of an afternoon he had spent at the Vendôme in Hollywood. Tables at the restaurant were dotted with pretty young starlets talking to noonday escorts, to directors, to fellow players. "But at one table," wrote Sobol, "I saw a group of drab-looking middle-aged women . . . like a cluster of Dubuque housewives on a tour. At the head of their table sat a woman, drab and lustreless as her companions—save for large, slumbrous eyes, which immediately arrested attention. No one was able to identify these people, except the one woman of the eyes . . . Theda Bara."

It was perhaps not quite fair to blame the one-time "reddest rose in hell" for allowing herself a retired life of ease and good works. The choice was hardly hers. Theda Bara had shot to the top in one breathtaking bolt, creating a vogue of vampires that swept the nation. She had remained there in splendid isolation, the sole support for almost all of her films (who today even remembers the names of her male leads, players such as Fritz Leiber, Thurston Hall, and Einar Linden?). She had tried to broaden her scope, but a relentless typecasting had forced her back again and again into the vampire mold. The vogue for wicked women, destroyers of men, reached an apex and then inevitably declined. Later, a second wave of vampires was to win favor, but for the moment the image had worn itself out.

The doom of the image was no doubt hastened by the end of

World War I. No longer was America menaced by forces from abroad. The evil, foreign-appearing seductress began to seem ludicrous in an era of serenity and good will, a time that formed the transition to the Jazz Age and the reign of the flapper. Locally, Hollywood was upset by the Fatty Arbuckle scandal and by handsome Wally Reid's untimely death as a result of dope addiction. Filmmakers, eager to avoid charges of courting sin and sensationalism, looked with sudden disfavor on the old-style melodramatic, panting, leering vampire.

Technical change, too, was transforming motion pictures. Yesterday's success often appeared archaic. As the twenties progressed, Theda Bara films already seemed old-fashioned, part of a bygone era. Occasional showings evoked laughter from audiences.

For Theda Bara there was really little left to do but to gather together good friends for dinner parties and, from time to time, to remind people of what it was like when she was one of filmdom's greatest stars.

"To understand those grand days, with the world of movies so new and all, you must consider that people believed what they saw on the screen," she told Hedda Hopper on a radio show. "Nobody had then destroyed the grand illusion. They thought the stars of the screen were the way they saw them. Nobody had knocked down any of their idols. Now they know it's all just make believe."

"It's the stars themselves who have been failing the fans," she said of the current favorites. "People have always been hungry for glamour—they still are. But it takes showmanship and a constant sense of responsibility to hold their interest. A star mustn't allow her public to see her in slacks. She should dress beautifully at all times—I don't mean in a bizarre way. She must live their dreams for them and remain a figure of mystery. Glamour is the most essential part of Hollywood."

On April 6, 1955, Theda Bara died of cancer after a year-long illness. Her aura of exotic mystery remained behind, and so did much of the extraordinary legend with which William Fox surrounded her. In its obituary the *New York Herald Tribune*

mistakenly informed readers that the archetype of wicked
screen sirens had begun her career in Paris at the Théâtre
Antoine. There, using the name De Coppet, she had delighted
Parisians for several years before going on to further sensational
triumphs in America, said the article.

Thus, a half century after the fact, it was difficult for even a
respected newspaper to distinguish between reality and her
studio's wondrous inventions. Perhaps that was not so surprising. The fiction, after all, was so much more fascinating than
the fact.

2

BARBARA LAMARR

THE
TOO-BEAUTIFUL
GIRL

Once upon a time, a young girl grew up in a small desert town in the West. Her parents, Mr. and Mrs. Watson, had given her an exotic first name, Reatha, and at an early age she began to live up to it. She had dreamy, expressive eyes, which seemed mysteriously sometimes to change in color, from deep gray to sea-green and even to a fleeting hint of purple. Dusky lashes added to their beauty. Reatha's nose and mouth were extremely fine, as perfect as if drawn by an artist. Her skin was soft and fair, and it contrasted happily with her dark, wavy hair, which she let trail to her shoulders. Everyone remarked upon her striking appearance, and her parents sometimes thought that she was almost too beautiful.

The family was glad to be living in an isolated little village in California's Imperial Valley. Seclusion would mean protection for their daughter. Only Reatha did not like the silent desert and the quiet life around her. Her imagination carried her to the city of Los Angeles, which she had heard was not very far away. There the streets were wide, the lights stayed on all night, and people danced and laughed and were gay. Reatha loved to

61

dance. Perhaps one day she would be a dancer. Or maybe an actress.

Her parents were ordinary hard-working people, who moved from place to place in the valley as employment became available. Reatha did not feel that she could talk to them of her dreams, so she put her visions into childish verse. Sometimes she imagined that they were not her parents at all, but that she was an adopted child, that her real parents were wonderful, romantic people from another, more exciting world. There was actually substance to this fantasy, Reatha later found. She was indeed a foster child. And it was true that living in the house with her was not her real sister but a step-sister. To her Reatha sometimes confided her frustrations and her hopes. One evening when Reatha was fifteen, the step-sister called her and told her to come quickly. Outside the house a car was parked with her boyfriend and another man. Reatha got in and drove off into the night. When the two girls had not returned the next day, the anxious parents called the police. Several days later Reatha was found on the outskirts of Los Angeles, bewildered, shaken, and unwilling to talk of her experiences.

When the case came up in court, a cub reporter named Adela Rogers St. Johns befriended Reatha, who was shy and frightened by this sudden notoriety. In her newspaper account of the case, Adela described Reatha's appearance, her dark blue serge sailor suit, her funny black poke bonnet, the ragged glove with which she at times touched her quivering lip. She also reported the words of the presiding judge, a kindly old man who leaned over and almost whispered to Reatha, "You're too beautiful to be alone in a big city while you're so young. Go back to the country, back to your folks. You're too beautiful, my child. You don't understand where it might lead you."

In the small valley town to which she reluctantly returned, the incident appeared to add to Reatha's attractiveness. The men of the area looked with ever-increasing interest at her young, graceful figure. They noted the full bosom, the long, slender, sensitive hands. More than ever the Watsons wondered if she was not, as the judge had said, too beautiful. Pensively they sent her to visit friends in nearby Arizona.

The magnet of her beauty glowed as powerfully there as it had at home. Riding by on his bronco, a big, raw-boned, bronzed young rancher was dazzled by this visitor to his planet. Again and again he rode by. When Reatha went for walks, he followed her at a distance. At night he often kept a vigil over the house in which she was staying. One day his pent-up passion found expression in action. Reatha and a girl friend were taking a spin across country in an automobile, and the young rancher drew alongside as they waited for a stop light. Without a word he lifted her up on his horse and rode off across the sands. The storybook tactics appealed to Reatha. She married her cavalier, whose name was Jack Lyttle. Only a few months later the apparently healthy rancher died of pneumonia, and his bride became a sixteen-year-old widow.

Reatha could not yet have known it, but a pattern was beginning to form. Her face, said Adela Rogers St. Johns, was "the kind that could no more go peacefully through a world of men than a cobblestone could pass through a plateglass window without busting things up." Still naive and restless, anxious to forget the past and athirst for a new life, the child widow went to Los Angeles. Almost immediately she met a handsome young lawyer named Lawrence Converse, and almost instantly they fell in love and were married.

At the simple wedding ceremony idealistic visions danced through the white-veiled bride's head. In addition to his good looks Converse had a prominent, cultivated family background. His far-ranging interests would evoke an eager response from her, an omnivorous reader of books. His established practice would provide security. At the wedding supper with her family Reatha radiated happiness, but unfortunately it was to be pathetically short-lived.

When the announcement of the marriage was printed in the papers, it brought a badly shaken woman to the district attorney's office. Her name, she said, was Mrs. Lawrence Converse. She and her three children were anxiously awaiting the missing father's return to the household. Under threat of arrest for bigamy, Converse went home, explaining in his own defense that on meeting Reatha her startling beauty had so haunted him that all thought of his past had been obliterated from his mind. Doctors were called in to examine the amnesia that the girl's spell had caused. They found that her face remained his constant obsession. A blood clot, they declared, was causing pressure on the brain and might result in a permanent mental disorder. The doctors operated to remove the clot. Their patient died on the operating table.

The distraught, broken-hearted Reatha went into hiding. Her worried foster father conducted a long search, which led eventually to a cheap boarding house. Here he found Reatha Watson sitting alone and expressionless, at her feet a newspaper that carried the story of her second husband's tragic death.

The too-beautiful girl was not yet eighteen, but her soft, soulful eyes reflected a depth of experience uncommon for that tender age. It had become impossible for Reatha to return to the family home. A strange nemesis seemed to pursue her, but each step of its unwinding seemed to play itself out on a larger stage. For a number of months she lived with her step-sister in Los Angeles, working as an interpretative dancer at clubs and theaters but unable to enjoy in any meaningful way the life of the city. Gradually her reputation grew. Engagements at cabarets and ballrooms around the country—as far afield as New York's Old Lincoln Hotel at Broadway and 52nd Street—brought her into contact with the many-faceted world of show business, with its customs and rituals, its varied characters, its exacting demands and rewards.

Blithely she succumbed again to a man, who pursued her with unrelenting ardor. Her third husband, Phil Ainsworth, a chorus dancer, belonged to that world that was gradually engulfing her. Their brief, unhappy marriage ended in divorce in 1917, when Reatha had just turned twenty. The following year she married comedian Ben Deely, a union that wound up once again in the divorce court. Yet once more the hapless Reatha marched to the altar, with red-haired serial player Jack Dougherty, from whom she eventually separated.

The piling up of experiences and marital failures had its

effect on the too-beautiful girl. Wherever she went, men continued to pursue her, but she was less spontaneous in her response. She studied the people she met and began to put her thoughts on paper. "No woman who has not known love can have a soul," she wrote. "Love *is* soul. But it is rarely a person we truly love. It is always the ideal of love we cherish as youngsters. Whenever anyone attracts us sympathetically, we bring from the lavender wrappings of our memories all of those ideals we had of the man our Prince Charming was to be, and drape them over the man before us."

For her new line of endeavor, writing, Reatha chose a new name, Barbara LaMarr. Blondes who turn brunette—or the reverse—often find that the new shade makes them feel different, adds a novel hue to their personality. Similarly, the change of name seemed to give fresh expression to the young writer's personality, to make her more outgoing and free. The Hollywood film colony was around the corner, parties were the order of the day, and at one of them Barbara LaMarr met the general manager of Fox Studios, Winfield Sheehan. She talked to him eagerly of her latest brainchild, a nearly completed novel. When Sheehan expressed interest and told her to make a scenario of it, Barbara left the party and went straight to work. The finished screenplay pleased Fox, and the studio produced it under the title *The Mother of His Children,* with Gladys Brockwell in the featured role.

Men had always been at Barbara's feet. Dancing had come naturally to those shapely limbs. Was it really surprising that writing should be as easy? Fox quickly put her on its payroll, and during the run of her contract she produced six more stories, which were also turned into films. In the process she became interested in acting. That, too, seemed fated, as did all that went with it: the swift success, the spectacular popularity, the horror.

Barbara LaMarr's film career began in 1921 with a role in *Paying the Piper,* which starred Anita Stewart. This led to a part with Harry Carey in *The Desperate Trail* and another with Douglas Fairbanks in *The Nut.* Pleased with her performance,

Fairbanks cast her as Milady de Winter in his production of *The Three Musketeers.* The role caught the attention of talented director Rex Ingram, who had an uncanny gift for picking embryonic stars. Ingram gave her the part of Antoinette de Mauban in *The Prisoner of Zenda*, a much-heralded film that was a vehicle for screen favorite Alice Terry, Ingram's wife. *The Prisoner of Zenda* was a huge success, bringing praise to all concerned but especially to two players whose startling good looks drew gasps from audiences: Barbara LaMarr and a sleek, dark-haired young Mexican boy named Ramon Samanegos, *alias* Novarro.

Director Ingram carefully noted the magic quality that crystallized on the screen in scenes between these two. He proceeded to give them star billing in *Trifling Woman*, for which he himself wrote the screenplay. The story dealt with a novelist and his daughter, who was breaking the heart of her fiancé by trifling with the affections of other men. To teach her a lesson the father wrote a novel that showed how destructive and purposeless the life of a coquettish adventuress really was. After reading the work the daughter came to her senses and, in turn, to the arms of her gentle and good fiancé.

Basically Ingram had written an old-fashioned Theda Bara-type vampire tale, the major variation in the pattern being the substitution of new stars for old. The slightly altered formula, complete with antique frame, worked. Several years had elapsed since Theda had last poured poison into the coffee of a victim, and in her absence Mary Pickford's golden curls and saccharine portrayals had continued to flood the screen. The public, which had tired of wicked old Theda's pyrotechnics, was now apparently ready to pay homage to Barbara LaMarr, who did her vamping in a more refined, almost languid style. The new vampire's name was as exotic sounding as Theda's, but she was nevertheless considered much more of a native product. "Home-made vampires are fully equal to the foreign," Barbara declared. Lines at the box office verified her judgment, and *Photoplay*, "The World's Leading Moving Picture Magazine," displayed her on its cover.

In rapid succession director Clarence Badger cast her in *Quincy Adams Sawyer,* and Fred Niblo put her into *Strangers of the Night.* She made *The Eternal Struggle* with the popular Wallace Beery. For George Fitzmaurice she went to Rome to film *The Eternal City,* which boasted an all-star cast headed by Lionel Barrymore, Richard Bennett, Bert Lytell, and Montague Love (as well as dictator Benito Mussolini and the King of Italy). *Thy Name Is Woman,* a Fred Niblo production presented by Louis B. Mayer under the Metro banner, reunited her with Ramon Novarro in a turbulent, sensual smuggling saga. *The Shooting of Dan McGrew,* based on Robert Service's famous poem of the Yukon gold fields, saw her playing "the lady known as Lou" with Lew Cody, Mae Busch, Eagle Eye, and child actor Philippe de Lacy.

Reporters of the period were often inclined to use the word "pretentious" to indicate a film's lofty aspirations and "picturization" in a sense roughly equivalent to adaptation. The picturization of the Service poem was highly melodramatic and pretentious, the scene shifting grandly from the South Seas to New York's glittering Great White Way and ending in Alaska, in the Malamute saloon made famous by the poet. The reception accorded its star, at this zenith of her career, reflected the varying judgments of her assets. Of her beauty there was never any question. Of her acting ability and of her sirenic characterizations there were mixed views.

From the *Herald Tribune's* Harriette Underhill came an encomium: "Never have we seen Miss LaMarr act better nor look so well. She seems to be getting more soulfully beautiful as time goes on."

"Barbara LaMarr earns her every closeup with some real dancing, real tears, and real acting," said the *Daily News.*

"Barbara LaMarr is a young woman so beautiful in full dress that it is difficult to . . . understand why she continues to go in for the disrobing scheme," said the reviewer for the *New York World.*

"While there is no denying Miss LaMarr's beauty, her characterization of Lou is singularly unimpressive," said the *New*

York Times. "It gives one the idea that she has not bothered much about the poem. Her overdoctored lips glisten in the glare of the klieg lights, and she indulges in her usual conception of excitement by panting."

There were those who felt that Barbara's quivering eyebrows behaved like untrained seals, and a sarcastic story circulating throughout Hollywood told of how directors put the star through her paces with commands like, "All right, Miss LaMarr, let's have expression number three now, if you please."

The man who wielded more power than even his New York counterparts, Edwin Schallert, the caustic critic for the *Los Angeles Times,* presented the prevailing opinion: that it was not great acting ability but rather incredible beauty radiating from a singular and disturbing personality that had sent Barbara LaMarr's star bolting to the heights of the film firmament in two short years. "She is made for lurking tragedy," wrote Schallert. "One feels the beat of ravens' wings about her. She mirrors even joy as would a deep tar. . . . Her radiance is that of moonlight in the heavy shadows of the night. . . . Calypso she is, burning with a flame of subtle ecstasy."

Elsie Ferguson, herself a great star of the period, was quoted as saying of the mysterious quality that drew people to Barbara LaMarr: "The real thing that has lifted her to the heights is, as any woman will tell you, the look in her eyes. The look in her eyes. Not the size of them, not their color, but the impenetrable something that lies in their depths. A something that is there because Barbara LaMarr would never accept placidly that which she might learn from others. Always she has sought thirstily for knowledge. Not as most of us seek, after the manner of our elders, but with a determination to learn for herself the pettiness and vastness of life. Ungovernable since childhood has been her curiosity. As each experience unfolded before her that insatiable quality has driven her on to a newer one. Subtle, enticing, vital. Mocking at civilization yet ultra-civilized.

"She is the vital pagan type to whom the game is ever worth the candle, and to whom every experience, mean or worthwhile, but serves to whet the appetite for more, to strengthen her

Lest your forget
Barbara La Marr

Barbara LaMarr

Barbara co-starred with Matt Moore in *Strangers of the Night,* 1923.

Barbara LaMarr and Lewis Stone in *Trifling Woman,* 1922.

"The Too-Beautiful
Girl" with Ramon No-
varro (left) and Stuart
Holmes in *The Prisoner
of Zenda,* 1922. The film
was a huge success.

On the set of *The Eternal Struggle,* 1923. Back row: Anders Randolph,
Wallace Beery, Reginald Barker, Joseph Swickard, George Kuwa. Front
row: Barbara LaMarr, Earle Williams, Renée Adorée, Pat O'Malley.

Barbara and players in *The Shooting of Dan McGrew*, based on Robert Service's famous poem about the Yukon gold fields. Barbara played "the lady known as Lou."

Barbara LaMarr's and Ramon Novarro's startlingly good looks drew gasps from audiences. They were paired here in *Thy Name Is Woman*.

Returning from Europe, 1924.

Barbara, born Reatha Watson, was visited on the set of her last film (1925) by her father.

Barbara and her adopted son, Ivan.

Barbara, her son, and her mother.

"Home-made vampires are fully equal to the foreign," declared Barbara. Audiences agreed.

Barbara defended accusations that she was an unfit mother. Here she attends a custody hearing in Los Angeles Superior Court.

Top: with her nurse outside the sanitarium in which she was treated for "nervous exhaustion." There were rumors that Barbara was becoming more and more dependent on drugs.

Left: returning to Hollywood after her recovery from what was reportedly a nervous breakdown.

A friend maintains a lonely vigil at the coffin of Barbara LaMarr, who died on January 30, 1926. Adela Rogers St. Johns, who christened Barbara "the too-beautiful girl," said, "She died because the tale was told."

personality and her belief that the fates alone determine our happiness. Like a lovely panther she is ... graceful, silky, always quiescent, yet ever with that primitive look of warning in the back of her lovely glowing eyes. That look that fascinates, lures, even while it warns of the danger of arousing her and brings a realization that beneath all this velvety softness are quickly unsheathable claws. That primitive fire that lurks so near the surface is, Barbara LaMarr herself believes, the basis of her appeal. And all of this is behind the look in her eyes."

As a child, Barbara LaMarr had worn cheap clothes and had sometimes gone hungry. Now that a stellar contract was in her lap, money flowed freely into her hands, and it was important to her for what it could buy: a richer, more varied, more generous life. "Why is it that rich men never seem to be attractive?" she lamented. "Is it that those qualities which makes it possible for them to acquire wealth make them unlovable?"

Barbara herself kept little account of her income; she kept the money in circulation. From one side of the lovely house she bought in Whitley Heights she could see Rudolph Valentino's first Hollywood home, while below, on Cahuenga Boulevard, lay leading man Jack Kerrigan's house. In typical Hollywood style, an enormous sunken bath dominated her all-onyx bathroom. The fixtures were, of course, solid gold.

Barbara liked to go to parties, and she loved to give them. When social gatherings had reached their peak of enjoyment, she, always mischievous, sometimes pulled a switch that shut off all the lights; then she bemoaned the fact that there was a power shortage. When her guests had profited by the darkness to assume somewhat intimate positions, she gleefully pulled the switch and surveyed their embarrassment.

Although Prohibition was calculated to put severe curbs on the nation's night life, it had in fact an almost contrary effect, and Barbara was one of those who enjoyed staying out until dawn. One night at New York's El Fay Club she spoke to her admirer, columnist Harriette Underhill. "Eat, drink, and be merry, for tomorrow we die," she declared. "This life is so short, and there are so many things to do. I must hurry." There was a sense of foreboding in the vivacious star, who frequently left checks for $25 as tips for the "ladies in waiting" at clubs she attended. Sleep was a little death. "To think that nature planned that we should spend one-third of our lives in a coma!" she said querulously. "Well, I've frustrated her. I seldom waste more than two hours out of twenty-four in sleep."

Barbara's life was a restless, whirling stampede. Work took its toll. "I think it would kill me to fail, to disappoint those who believe in me," she declared. "I love every moment of the work I have done, love every inch of progress I have made. But every characterization I give the screen takes a chip off the edge of my very soul, makes me just a little older."

No one was surprised that the hard playing, hard working young actress spent money freely, went to clubs, stayed up late, and drew columns of newspaper space. The Roaring Twenties were beginning. A little later Clara Bow was to become the symbol of that fast-moving age, but Barbara LaMarr anticipated her. Her candor continually startled reporters, who seldom printed what she actually said. Her lust for life was a part of the spirit of the times. What did surprise many was that almost as soon as she had enough money to feel secure, she adopted a baby.

While in Texas on a personal appearance tour, Barbara turned away from the applause and adulation of her fans, quietly made her way to Hope Cottage, a foundling home in Dallas, and walked out with a sixteen-month-old baby, a boy with great blue eyes and tangled yellow curls. The child had won her heart on sight. "I adopted a baby because I wanted something to love. And the only thing I've found in this world that is at all satisfactory to love is a baby," she said.

Clothes, jewels, servants, success, admiration, and wealth, all these must make her life seem thrilling and romantic, she said, but in actuality she felt in her mouth the taste of ashes. The world around her seemed hollow, the attentions often proved to be insincere, and the greatest danger of all was an absorption with self. At the age of twenty-six she could write: "I've had wisdom thrust upon me until it isn't hard for me to look ahead to a loveless, lonely old age. When what they are pleased to call my beauty is faded, when they've forgotten the tinkle of this thing called fame, and my name is wiped from the slate of the world's favor, when money will only buy you hats you can't wear and food you can't eat, then—you want somebody to love you."

Barbara LaMarr had been a foster child. She knew the loneliness that comes from having no one that seemed truly to belong to her. Into her house she was bringing a nameless, homeless atom and giving it a name and a home. She was making a bargain, trying to insure her life, trying to buy love with love, trying very candidly to buy it from a baby, not from men. "I am sick of men, the admiration of men, the so-called love of men," she declared. "I have been married. I have known some little about men in my life. Men's love is most unsatisfactory, the most disillusioning thing in life. The little girl who has only one beau, who grows up and marries him and keeps her ignorance and her faith in men is the lucky girl. Not the woman whom the world may call fortunate because men flock to her feet. . . . The admiration, the desire of men leaves you stranded on a sea of fear and loneliness and self-loathing. That's why I adopted a boy. I know perhaps enough of men and the world and the temptations of the world to bring him up to be the man I always wanted to marry but never could find. . . ."

Early and late, Barbara had searched for her ideal, a man whose qualities she could never quite define, perhaps because they were those imagined perfections of the real father she had never known. Long after she had given up the search, men continued to try to break through to her heart, and each new experience left her with more ashes in her mouth, with more distrust. "Barbara is the eternal contradiction," said Ben Lyon, one of her leading men. "Love to her is a torture, always a torture, and yet I think she must have drunk some love philtre, for she cannot help loving any more than men can help loving her. There is intoxication in every line of her, every sound of her voice. She is Circe, but she is never happy. No one, I think, has ever seen Barbara happy. Joyous, laughing, merry, wild with delight, yes. Oh, yes. But never just happy."

In her films Barbara played the vampire, the woman who has a fatal attraction for men and uses it to achieve her own ends. In real life she exercised that same fascination, much against her own will. "I seem always to be cast in parts where love is my whole existence. Even life has done that to me," Barbara herself said. "Perhaps it is because I've always been in love, in love with the great ideal of love itself—something that too many men and women experience, something that makes us go on seeking through personalities and the years. The world calls us fickle, but that isn't true. We are merely the idealists of love, who search and very rarely find that for which we look. . . ."

In Hollywood the idealistic too-beautiful girl was noted for her impulsiveness, her swift changes of mood, her quick flights of temper, which she sometimes attributed to what she called "my wop blood." She was known for her warmth and extraordinary feeling of tolerance, for her desire to please other people, to make them happy. It was said that Barbara LaMarr could never say no. At the height of her career that fatal beauty, which had drawn her helplessly into premature sorrows, dealt her a terrifying new blow.

A complex series of legal steps provided a prelude. Several years earlier, after she had been divorced from her third husband in Chicago, she had gone on to marry Ben Deely. Subsequently, she had learned that the Chicago divorce was invalid, and in consequence she considered her marriage to Deely automatically annulled. This, she felt, left her free to marry Jack Dougherty, her fifth husband. To test by law whether he had ever been legally married to Barbara, Deely brought a divorce complaint against her. As his counsel he employed Herman Roth, a fairly well-known Hollywood attorney. According to Deely, the complaint at this stage contained no names and no direct innuendo against anyone's reputation.

Roth, however, prepared an amended divorce complaint, which contained a direct charge of misconduct against Barbara, naming some thirty-six men, many notable in the movie colony. Roth brought the amended complaint to the attention of producer Arthur Sawyer, to whom Barbara was under contract, and asked for $20,000 in hush money in exchange for a promise not to give the story to a Los Angeles newspaper. Recognizing Roth's criminal intent, Sawyer cleverly arranged to trap him by paying him in marked bills before witnesses. He then informed police of the attempted extortion. When Roth was brought to trial, a Los Angeles jury took exactly eight minutes to return a guilty verdict.

The marriage to Dougherty survived the legal onslaught but not the divisive career factor. "Why I Quit Being Mr. Barbara LaMarr," the comedian later wrote in a bylined article, explaining that the male ego could not cope with the idolatry accorded a wife who was famous.

The immediate question after the trial, however, was whether the career of Barbara LaMarr would survive the scandal of the courtroom. After the trials of comedian Fatty Arbuckle on rape-murder charges and the death of movie idol Wallace Reid, film producers had begun inserting morality clauses into their contracts. A key paragraph stated in no uncertain terms that the contracts were binding only so long as "the party of the first part," the star, remained "free from scandal." Producer Sawyer had inserted such a clause into the LaMarr contract.

The option to renège on the contract was not exercised. The vivid, dark, exotic, and alluring beauty of Barbara LaMarr continued to fill the silent screen, looming larger, more impressive even than in life. For First National she made *The White Moth* with Conway Tearle. *Sandra* rolled off the assembly line, along with *Arabian Love*, co-starring handsome John Gilbert. Tearle and Clifton Webb surrounded Barbara in *The Heart of a Siren*, an impossible story that nonetheless found favor with the public. In one scene the siren glances at one poor man, who is immediately seized with an incurable infatuation. He tosses a rose to her, and the dazzling woman treads on it. Stupidly, the afflicted one follows her upstairs unbidden. Looking into her half-open, indifferent eyes he realizes that he means nothing in her life, pulls out a pistol, and puts a bullet through his head. A moment later the siren calmly asks a servant, "How dare you allow people to kill themselves at my door?" When the siren herself finally develops an affection that is not returned, she determines to take poison—not, however, before changing into an insinuating satin gown, the appropriate costume for the occasion.

The product somehow pleased. From Europe came vampires Pola Negri and Lya De Putti. Dagmar Godowsky and Brooklyn's Nita Naldi were exercising their wiles upon the screen, but for a few brief halcyon years Barbara LaMarr was in the forefront of public favor as the embodiment of sirenic allure. When in August, 1925, *Photoplay*'s Herbert Howe started handing out golden apples to the ten most beautiful women in Hollywood, her name shone in the list next to such favorites as Corinne Griffith, Marion Davies, and Norma Shearer.

Even as the magazine appeared on the stands, newspapers informed their readers that Barbara LaMarr was seriously ill. The Roth trial had been like a festering sore, drawing poison to its center. All the forces that had charged the glittering young actress's life with an unnatural intensity now coalesced for a final surge. The pace of film production continued unabated. A disturbed Barbara hurried to New York to make *The White Monkey*; then she rushed back to the West Coast to begin *The Girl from Montmartre*. In New York her private life had kept pace with her work schedule, and her favorite clubs noted that she was often the last person to leave before they closed their doors. A different escort accompanied her each evening. Lovers, she said, one should have like roses—by the dozen.

For a time her graceful figure became strangely heavy, the coloring of her once pearl-white skin a sickly pallor. There was talk of overindulgence, persistent whispers of drugs. Indeed, dope of every kind was said to be part of the LaMarr repertory—opium of the finest grade Benares, cocaine exotically housed in a golden model casket on the grand piano. Early and late, Bobby—the name her close friends called her—tasted life in all its aspects.

A relentless diet brought back the graceful lines of the too-beautiful girl, but it took a merciless toll on her constitution.

Back in Hollywood Barbara lived alone, having separated from the red-haired Dougherty. As filming began on *The Girl From Montmartre*, she called on her foster father, who had stood by her so often in the past, to come to her help. Each day he drove with her to the studio in her Rolls Royce, acquired at the height of her sudden fame. Her work schedule was reduced to three or four hours a day, but even so she fainted on the set again and again from sheer weakness. For those who remembered the vibrant, fun-loving Barbara of other days, the thin, pale specter trying to smile her old mesmeric smile was a pitiful sight.

The heavy cost of physicians and medicines suddenly gave money a significance it had never had before in the haggard star's life. To her dismay she found that she was already drawn ahead on her salary to the extent of $60,000. Mundane items such as savings accounts and rainy days had never interested her. Now, one by one, she released her household staff. Admirers and hangers-on disappeared. One Saturday afternoon in October Barbara collapsed again on the set, and her doctors ordered her to give up work until she regained strength. Filming was completed, but it was a critically ill star who retreated to a mountainside sanitarium.

The film colony knew that Barbara LaMarr was waging a fight for her life. No visits from studio friends were permitted, however. No word came of progress or decline. Only those closest to her knew that Barbara had put her adopted son, Donald, into the care of a dear friend, Mrs. Tom Gallery, better known as actress Zasu Pitts, and made provisions for his upbringing. It was perhaps the fatalistic Barbara's way of prophesying a known end. Although she made a brief recovery, adding eight pounds to her fragile frame and moving to her foster parents' home in Altadena, a sudden relapse ended her life on Saturday, January 30, 1926. Again there were whispers of dope, of an overdose.

"In movie circles they say that Barbara LaMarr committed suicide," wrote one reporter. "Not that she actually and willingly killed herself by her own hand. But she did deliberately shut her eyes to danger and plunge on to her death. And months before anyone else knew that Barbara was ill, the star herself knew that she was going to die."

The woman who had christened her the too-beautiful girl, Adela Rogers St. Johns, said more simply: "She died because the tale was told."

Certain it is that a fire raged inside the heart of the captivating actress, raged with such intensity that it early burned itself out. "She is of a nervous temperament, and you must drive her as you would drive a nervous horse, with a light yet firm rein," wrote one of her directors, Fred Niblo. "She is always so sweet and smiling and gracious that you cannot be sure whether the part is actually working out as she sees it. . . . There is a lack of force there, of that divine discontent that drives us to bigger things. Too easy to please, too anxious to please. Yet those are the very things that give her that velvety sensuous softness on the screen, smothering thinking in a gentle, dreamy appeal."

"The sweetness of her, the sheer, overpowering, tender sweetness of her. The infinite promise of delight," co-star Ben Lyon had said.

All over now, the tale nevertheless seemed to have no end. Barbara had died intestate, debt-ridden. Years after her death her third husband was convicted of forgery and sent to Folsom prison. The last man to share her life, Virgil Jack Dougherty, was found dead of carbon monoxide poisoning in a parked automobile in Hollywood Hills in 1938. Prison, suicide, madness, premature and sudden death, all the classic fruits of the vampire's mania came to those who loved Barbara LaMarr. She would not have wanted it so, to see her quality of beauty become a curse.

That strange enchantment was not easily forgotten even in Hollywood, where beauties were almost as common as orange trees. Barbara LaMarr's body was placed in state, and more than 40,000 admirers filed past the bier. In Hollywood Cemetery, where services were to be held, hundreds came to the chapel, and police were forced to battle the throng that clamored for seats. One woman fought so desperately for a view of the casket that she was forcibly removed. Five others fainted and were barely saved by police from being trampled by the crowd. In accordance with the too-beautiful girl's wishes, the simple ceremonies were conducted by a reader of the Christian Scientist church. They had been delayed for several days because commitments had kept director Paul Bern in New York. Bern had long ago lost his heart to Barbara LaMarr, and during her illness he was one of the few permitted to communicate with her. Now he sat in the front row, tears staining his face. He was to find love again several years later with another actress, and when that love turned sour he was, in desperation, to commit suicide. The actress was another beautiful girl, a blonde named Jean Harlow.

3

POLA NEGRI

THE WILDCAT

It was a brilliant, sunny day in the late fall of 1922. As the transatlantic liner *Majestic* entered New York harbor, a boat especially chartered by Adolph Zukor, president of Paramount Pictures, sailed out to meet her. On board a band blared forth the Polish national anthem, and giant banners proclaimed, "Welcome Pola Negri." Socialites and politicians were ignored as the *Majestic* docked. Reporters, photographers, passengers, and spectators swarmed in tumultuous welcome around the first big movie star to be imported into the country.

Fabulous Pola Negri, the temperamental European actress, lived up to her elaborate advance publicity. As porters struggled with her twenty-seven trunks, a French maid shouted imprecations in broken English. Pola herself stood in regal splendor, ringed by admirers, and sputtered forth exclamations of joy in her native Polish. She wore a stunning Cossack dress. High Russian boots and a turban made her appear taller than her actual five feet, six inches. When for a moment she lifted the turban in a gesture of salute to New York, everyone saw the

81

lustrous jet-black hair, which fell in bangs almost to her eyebrows. Her luminous dark eyes were framed by heavily made-up brows and lashes, while her skin was startlingly white by contrast. A small sequined mole at the corner of the left eye served as a beauty mark. If the reporters had difficulty coping with la Negri's mixture of Polish, English, Russian, French, and German, the photographers at least were having a field day.

A motorcycle police caravan soon escorted the star through the streets to her hotel. After a brief rest, the triumphal first day in America continued with a gala soirée in her honor at the Ritz, where 300 guests were invited for a Viennese dinner. Each course was accompanied by its appropriate wine or champagnes, no small feat during Prohibition, when bathtub gin and vintage shellac constituted a connoisseur's cache. Cost for the rare liquors, found by enterprising Paramount minions in a small East Side hideaway, amounted to more than $5,000, a figure that Adolph Zukor okayed, saying it was worth it to "keep the little lady happy."

As the evening wore on, a bejeweled and ermined Pola was taken to the Ziegfeld *Follies*. From the stage, Will Rogers sent her an affectionate greeting as the spotlight played over "the little lady," who bowed and cried with joy. The evening ended with a late supper given for her by Florenz Ziegfeld and his wife, Billie Burke.

For a glorious week Pola Negri was the toast of New York, fêted at luncheons, dinners, and theater parties, but then it was time to take the Twentieth-Century Limited for the West Coast and the film capital of the world. A vision in brown from silken turban to soft suede shoes, Pola was swathed in a magnificent sable wrap when she arrived in Chicago and granted another of an endless series of interviews. One of the first questions was about Charlie Chaplin, whom she had met several months earlier in Berlin and with whom she was reportedly having a romance.

"I think Charlie Chaplin is the most perfect nice moving picture actress is in the screen," she declared in her deep, heavily accented voice.

"Actress?" someone blurted.

"Absolute," said the smiling star. "The most perfect actress. Anglish nice, and Charlie Chaplin, she is nice, too."

On arrival in Hollywood another brass band was on hand, and flowers enough to fill a greenhouse added to the festive scene. Pola was enchanted when a little newsboy handed her a bouquet of roses. At a midday luncheon film pioneer Jesse Lasky invited only writers, having heard that Pola was a "well-read intellectual." The main subject of conversation, however, was her enormous solitaire diamond. The carnival atmosphere continued as Pola and her maid were taken to the Ambassador Hotel and installed in a spacious bungalow. Pola was told that she would appear that night as Cleopatra in a benefit pageant at the Hollywood Bowl. Afterward there was to be a supper in her honor at the Cocoanut Grove.

To *Photoplay*, via an interpreter, Pola conveyed her message to America: "Always America has been my dream from the time I was a child in Poland. You do not know how Polish children look toward America. It is like heaven to which people go for eternal happiness. The leaves of the trees are gold. Always people return rich or send money back. Everything is free and all people friendly.... For me America has been the fairy godmother, as wonderful, more wonderful than I could have imagined as a child. How could I ever have dreamed that America would one day love me? It was wonderful—in one night almost I hear that America is praising me and wanting me...."

Despite the outward signs of gaiety, clouds were to be seen on the horizon. It was hot, very hot, and humid. Pola found the climate oppressive. How would it be possible to work, to give her all in such a climate? And she needed a cook. A Polish cook. "One must eat," the mysterious, monosyllabic Pole told Paramount executives, who hurriedly scoured the environs to meet her demand.

At the Hollywood Bowl pageant a crowd of 20,000 cheered the sumptuously gowned new star. Director George Fitzmaurice told her that he was to direct her first film, and that his wife, novelist Ouida Bergere, was doing the screenplay. Pola in turn asked the director whether Charlie Chaplin might show up during the evening. Fitzmaurice said that the great comedian never made public appearances.

Pola was momentarily disappointed. She remembered her first meeting with Chaplin, some six months earlier, in Berlin, where she was a reigning film star and he a visiting celebrity. Mutual friends, the Albert Kauffmans, had brought them together and taken them to the Palais Heinroth, a fashionable restaurant. Pola had only heard distant echoes of Chaplin's American triumphs and squandered her English as she called him "little jazz-boy Charlie." He in turn asked the Kauffmans to tell her how much he admired her acting ability. Mischievously, Albert Kauffman translated his sentiment as "I think you are a piece of cheese." Intimations of homicide lurked in Pola's eyes until the true translation was given. On learning that Chaplin had praised her, she obligingly told him he was one of the world's great artists, and the rest of the party went off with everyone in good spirits.

Pola and Chaplin had met several times more, but their relationship had not progressed beyond friendship. They had promised to meet again in Hollywood. Now as her limousine carried her to the Cocoanut Grove supper party, Pola felt that perhaps it would not be soon and possibly that was for the best. In their brief time together she had seen in Chaplin a wistfulness, a sadness that stirred something inside her.

Suddenly her thoughts were interrupted by the movement of the car as it crashed into another limousine and lurched off the road. The car was traveling at slow speed, and no one was hurt. To Pola's astonishment the man who got out of the other car was Charlie Chaplin.

Just as it might have happened in a Hollywood screenplay, Pola got into Chaplin's car, thinking he would take her to the supper party. Chaplin had other thoughts, however. Without hesitation he declared his love and was headed straight for her bungalow at the Ambassador when further melodrama intervened. Rounding a slow winding curve, two gunmen jumped on the running board and threatened Chaplin. Since he was carrying only checks, it was Pola's bag, containing fifty dollars in cash, which appeased the holdup men. At her insistence, Chaplin drove to the party, refusing, however, to let her dance with Fitzmaurice or leading man Rod la Rocque when they asked her. As soon as he was able to get her away, he took her to her bungalow. During the course of the evening he told her about his early life, reducing her to tears with the stories of his sad London childhood, its poverty and cruelties, the illness of his mother, the despair that filled his young days.

When Chaplin finally left, a deeply moved Pola closed her eyes and hoped for the restorative sleep that would enable her to report for work at the studio in the morning. Just as she was dozing off she heard a crescendo of music and looked out to see a twenty-piece Hawaiian band, which the romantic Chaplin had sent to serenade her. Mustering all of her English, Pola begged the musicians to stop, but in vain. The band played on.

At Paramount everyone was waiting on the set for the appearance of the new star. Director Fitzmaurice, featured players, and extras were standing by. Executives chewed anxiously on expensive cigars. Ten o'clock came, then eleven and twelve, but no Pola. Finally at noon the phone rang, and a voice of undecipherable nationality said, "Madame Negri has the misfortune to have a toothache; she will not appear today."

So they were true, those stories of the fiery, temperamental Pole, studio bigwigs pondered fearfully. Editor Herbert Howe had said that the two greatest spectacles in Europe were Mount Etna and Pola Negri. When he had visited Pola at the Hotel Adlon in Berlin, he had been told two days in a row that the star was ill and begged to be excused. In Berlin, Howe learned, she was called "the wildcat" because of her running battles with co-workers and servants.

For a mountain scene in a German film of *Carmen*, director Ernst Lubitsch had told Pola to wear a skirt, but she had insisted on pants and appeared with them on set. "Go take off those pants," Lubitsch had ordered, but the irate actress, feeling the gypsy blood coursing through her veins, pulled a dagger from her costume belt and flew at the director. Lubitsch grabbed her wrist and forced her to drop the dagger. Seconds later she was begging his forgiveness, explaining that she had flown into a rage that left her not herself.

A common sight at the Adlon suite was that of a maid hurtling out of the star's dressing room to the accompaniment of ringing curses and assorted objets d'art. Within the hour the rage would pass, and Pola would appear in tears, declaring that she could not go on until her trusted old servant came back to her. Familiar with this routine, the hotel management would call the maid, who was usually playing pinochle with a group of waiters while waiting for her mistress to have a change of heart.

Paramount was well aware of Pola's reputation for towering tantrums, but they thought they could be managed. They were willing to make that try because of the star's record of artistic achievement. From her native Poland, where she had built a glowing career on the legitimate stage, la Negri had entrained for Berlin during the last years of World War I. Playing for the celebrated Max Reinhardt at the Kammerspiele Theater, she had recreated her 1912-1913 Warsaw stage role as the star of *Sumurun*, an Arabian Nights fantasy. Playing a dancing girl, the Slave of Fatal Enchantment, she lured all men who loved her to great tragedy. Her leading man was Emil Jannings, a sheik who bought her at a slave market. Ernst Lubitsch, a young actor also of Polish extraction, played an old woman, a grotesque character in pantomime. When the sheik's son falls in love with the slave girl, his infatuation becomes so great that he kills his father to win her. Pola's performance in *Sumurun* had drawn a standing ovation on opening night and praise from the major critics of Europe.

Her success on stage led to an immediate film offer from UFA (Universum Film Aktiengesellschaft), the big production company subsidized by the German state, which recognized the value of films for morale and propaganda purposes. At a salary twenty times higher than her theater wage, Pola made a bad little picture called *The Polish Dancer*; next she made *The Yellow Ticket*, only a little better.

As the time neared for her to start her third film, she remembered her former co-actor, Ernst Lubitsch, who had gone on from his acting role to direct several one- and two-reel comedies. Lubitsch's understanding of character development had impressed Pola. To Paul Davidson, UFA's general manager, she stated that she must have Lubitsch as the director of her next film. When Davidson was understandably reluctant to employ a comedy director for a dramatic actress, Pola put on a little histrionic display calculated to move him. After the emotional outburst she retired to her elaborate dressing room, a showplace all in white with walls of mirrors and rows of lights from floor to ceiling. There she contemplated UFA's iniquities.

Davidson gave in. Lubitsch directed Pola in *The Eyes of the Mummy*, a big money-maker, and in *Carmen*, also a great success. With another director, Paul Stein, Pola made a version of *Camille*, (later released in the United States as *The Red Peacock*); then Lubitsch, Emil Jannings, and Pola were reunited in her most extraordinary European film success, *DuBarry*. Lubitsch directed this story, of the beautiful little Paris milliner whom the world came to know as DuBarry, the mistress of a great king, while Jannings took the role of Louis XIV.

Pola became the most popular actress in Europe, but American distributors remained reluctant to import films from Germany, which had only recently been the country's wartime enemy. *DuBarry* made the rounds and was knocking about for months until it was picked up by S.L. Rothafel, an impresario better known as "Roxy," who later built the motion picture theater of that name in New York. Rothafel retitled his purchase *Passion* and booked it into New York's Capitol Theater.

The sensational reception accorded the film surprised everyone, including Rothafel. On December 15, 1920, an estimated 40,000 people jammed the streets around the theater, trying to gain entrance for the opening performance. Although presumably it is the largest motion picture house in the world, the Capitol's capacity was only 5,500 seats. Emergency police were called to handle the overflow when ticket sales were suspended, at six o'clock in the evening. For the next week, *Passion* played five performances a day, with a total of well over 100,000 admissions, bowling over all Capitol records, including that just set by Douglas Fairbanks' *The Mark of Zorro.* Rothafel had paid $40,000 for the American rights. *Passion* was now worth an estimated half million dollars.

The efforts of Lubitsch and Jannings were appropriately praised, but the magnet that drew the populace through the turnstiles was recognized to be the film's star. "Pola Negri is an actress of unusual appeal. She looks a bit like Theda Bara," said Agnes Smith in the *New York Morning Telegraph.* "Her main attractiveness lies in the contour of her face and the remarkably large and expressive eyes," said the *Evening Mail.* "As an actress she has a vivacity, a radiance, which endows the historic character of Madame DuBarry with life. . . . Her power and versatility as an emotional actress are reached by no American screen star I can call to mind. She is lovely, possessed of a beauty that combines vivacity and intelligence with the charm of perfect contour," reported the *Daily News.*

The *New York Times* was unreserved in its praise: "Here is one of those rare persons with screen personality. Her moving photograph is stamped with individuality. And largely because of her definite pantomimic ability or whatever distinctive motion picture acting may be called. It is not physical beauty that wins for her. She is lovely in many scenes, it is true, but some of her features are not too beautiful, and she makes no apparent effort to pose becomingly without regard to the meaning of her performance. She is expressive. That is her charm. She makes DuBarry real, as far as she has to be, with as much of the appearance of dignity as she must have on occasion, and as contemptuous and cowardly as she was. She actually wins sympathy for a person who cannot at any time be admired. This is an accomplishment."

Fan mail from America began reaching the elated Pola in Berlin. One effusive letter, written in a firm, attractive hand, bore the signature "Rudolph Valentino." For some reason she saved it.

When Pola's earlier film, *Carmen,* was released in the United

States as *Gypsy Blood* and turned a heavy profit, Adolph Zukor decided to import the European star. Let her play royal courtesans and wayward gypsies in Hollywood, and let the money from the box office flow into an American studio. As for temper, surely that could be handled, since there was a good deal of it around already.

Reigning stars Mary Pickford, Douglas Fairbanks, Charlie Chaplin, and director D.W. Griffith, had recently gone so far as to set up their own producing organization. The asylum was now in the hands of the lunatics, people were saying. One more addition to the asylum could hardly make much difference.

As it happened, Pola was not one more addition to the asylum. She was a match for the forces that prevailed, and the clash was something like an immovable object meeting an irresistible force.

On her second day in Hollywood, Pola arrived on schedule at the studio, her maid trailing behind. She was shown to her dressing room, whose red, black, and gold Chinese motif had been chosen by Mary Pickford when she was the queen of the studio, before "America's Sweetheart" left to go into independent production. Pola looked things over and mumbled something to her maid that was later found to be a Slavic equivalent for "must be completely done over."

Leaving the premises, the emotional star's eyes fell on a sight that made her evoke a loud scream—a black cat dashed across her path and out of sight. Although filming was scheduled to begin, Pola, profoundly superstitious, bounded back into her dressing room and refused to reappear until she was convinced that property boys had caught every cat on the lot. The black cat was a very bad omen for her, she felt. And the day was hot, another scorcher.

Still, there was nothing to do but return to the cat-free lot. The next horror was that she was expected to perform right out in the open, on the lot. In Germany UFA had closed in the area where she expressed the emotions required for her films. Surely in rich America she could make that simple request. How could she be expected to act while prop boys were wandering by and other unknown visitors peered curiously at her? It was unthinkable. Giving instructions to her maid on the new furnishings needed for the dressing room, Pola headed for her limousine.

Driving home in the studio-furnished car, she noted the elaborate vehicles that passed her on the road. Something would obviously have to be done about that. There was no point to coming all the way from Berlin to find yourself playing second fiddle. Pola sketched out the design of the automobile in which she would soon be seen about town: a very long Rolls Royce of pure white, trimmed with ivory and upholstered in white velvet, all this to contrast with her jet black hair and dark eyes. There would be a chauffeur who wore white uniforms on sunny days, black when it rained; a white lap dog would be needed and two white Russian wolf hounds; the horn should be in the form of a snake's golden head, the eyes set with rubies from that nice shop she had visited in New York, Cartier's. Solid gold door handles and fixings would add a nice finishing touch.

Feeling a little better by the time she arrived at her bungalow, Pola found a flood of messages awaiting her—invitations to dinners and parties, flowers from her little jazz-boy Charlie. They did love her in America after all. That evening she unpacked some of her jewelry, including a ninety-eight carat emerald bracelet, several large diamond rings, and a diamond necklace, and wore them to a dinner and several late-evening parties. She wore a stunning evening dress and indulged in a petite fantasie—she painted her nails red. At each gathering she was greatly admired, but, Pola found, the food was not very good. She was used to the international cuisine of Berlin, and when dishes were not properly seasoned, it ruined her mood. And the conversation—what she could understand of it—was focused on movies. Now a little bit of that was all right, but the entire evening! What about books, art, and music? After all, in Berlin she had designed her own clothes for her films. She had studied sculpture with a pupil of the great Rodin.

Pola left the last party before anyone else. On her way she realized that this hot, monotonously sunshiny town might very well be lonely for her. The thing was to get a pet, an animal that would be real company. A nice handsome tiger would do. They could take long walks together. Tomorrow she would see about it.

At the studio the next day Pola found that progress on one front was canceled out by more unpleasantness on another. The set was boxed in, but what did director Fitzmaurice want her to do—change the famous black and white mask of her face that had brought her fame throughout Europe? It was unthinkable. There was nothing to do but retire to the dressing room, though that was as yet in no livable condition. Pola tried to calm down, to remember the time that mask had developed.

Her career had begun on the legitimate stage, and when she first went before the cameras, she had made herself up very heavily, as usual. The rushes showed that what worked for the stage did not work for the screen. Dark shadows clouded her face. When the director took away all her greasepaint, she had felt a moment of panic. Then she found that a box of white talcum had been forgotten. She applied this. With a burnt match she darkened the area around her eyes, the lashes, the eyebrows, and the mole, which already stood out but not quite enough. To everyone's surprise the result was magnificent and startling.

Now this man Fitzmaurice wanted her to change, saying the white makeup crossed by the heavy level eyebrows at the top and the wide mouth at the bottom made the face too broad. "In Poland we kill!" the fuming Pola bellowed in her deep accented voice. Outside Fitzmaurice sent an assistant to explain that he only wanted to experiment. If the changes were not mutually satisfactory, they would be dropped. The trembling lackey conveyed the message and found the star immediately compliant. Pola knew that the changes would not be *mutually* acceptable. For a day at the studio she appeared in less contrasting makeup and completely upset a bevy of starlets on the lot, who had admired her and dropped their buxom complexions in favor of her ghostly white pallor slashed at the southern end with two vivid, startling lips. The following day they were further confused. Just as they had switched back to their normal contours, the treacherous Pola reappeared, smiling broadly through her black and white mask.

For her American debut the studio had chosen *Bella Donna*, a successful stage melodrama, populating it with Pola, Conway Tearle, Conrad Nagel, Adolphe Menjou, and Lois Wilson. Pola's role was that of a fascinating but unscrupulous woman who marries a young man (Nagel) for his prospective wealth and title; then she wearies of his goodness when a sensuous Oriental (Tearle) casts his spell upon her. She becomes a modern Lucrecia Borgia, about to kill her husband, but his physician friend arrives in time to discover her infamy and save him. In a tragic finale, Bella Donna, cast out by the man for whom she has attempted the crime, is left to face the desert, in which the howls of creeping beasts of prey mingle with the roar of an approaching sandstorm.

The tale was a very sinewy one, and Pola was eager to do it justice, to show every facet of this vicious vampire—her intoxicating allure and her heartless and ugly inner nature. In her European films she had never hesitated to present herself in an unflattering light if the role called for it. Now she was repeatedly asked to soften her characterization, to make Bella Donna less repellent. Each effort in this direction threw Pola into a towering rage. She was told that the exhibitors would not accept too vicious a heroine; the audiences would stay away. They had not stayed away from her no-holds barred interpretations in her European triumphs, she reminded one and all. But to no avail.

Again and again the fiery Pola would retire to her dressing room to sulk. Each return brought new confrontations. Some days the thought of going to work made her nauseous. She would have someone call the studio with what became a fairly familiar set of messages: "Miss Negri does not feel like today to work," "Miss Negri is seeck and will not be able to work today." Sometimes the message read, "Miss Negri has a toothache." Each of her perfect set of teeth must have ached at least once during the filming of *Bella Donna*. When it wasn't an indisposition, it was the climate that brought things to a standstill.

At work nothing irritated Pola more than the inefficiency of the studio routine. For hours she would be asked to sit and wait while props were pulled into position, cameras properly focused, final touches put to the positioning of extras. The Americans did not realize that one did not make a star wait; the imperious Pola found a solution to the problem. She installed herself in her dressing room, with its elaborate set of perfume bottles, books, and works of art, and there she remained while from time to time her maid reconnoitered the set to see where things stood. When the cameras were actually ready to start rolling, Madame Negri would make her appearance.

Music helped too. Pola auditioned a list of violinists until she found one to her taste. As she emoted before the glaring klieg lights, the court musician would play the melodies that set her mood.

And what was music without a little stimulant? After a scene was filmed, Pola found it refreshing to retire to her dressing room and have a sip or two of champagne. Momentarily she experienced a bad shock when told that the United States had something called Prohibition, that liquor was illegal, that federal officers were on the lookout for violators of the law. The appearance of a strange man around the set would throw terror into Pola's usually fearless heart, and for several days she would pass up her bracer. Then the taste for the proper way to do things would reassert itself, and she would calm her volatile spirit with a bit of Mumm's or a glass of chianti, chartreuse, or cognac.

Occasionally her attendants would forget to stock the larder, and a tired Pola would be forced to drink some rotgut procured in a hurry. At such moments she would put into practice her knowledge of curses and vitriol in four languages and hurl a perfume bottle or two at the offender for good measure. The storm might last for an hour or for a day. At its end, an exorcised Pola would reconcile with her servant and hand her a gift, usually fifty dollars.

One of the things that most infuriated Pola was the inability of most people to understand her. She would try to express herself in English; then seeing she was getting nowhere, she would try Polish, French, and German, to the increasing bewilderment of her listeners. When all failed, she would shout one of her favorite invectives or that old battle-cry: "In Poland we kill!"

Her lack of English could work to her advantage. In the middle of a scene she would stop after having finished a semi-closeup. "Now a beeg head," she would tell the cameraman and her director, who would find it difficult to refuse her simple appeal.

Despite her artistic disagreements, Pola liked her Irish-French director, George Fitzmaurice. He and his wife Ouida maintained perhaps the most literate household in Hollywood, and they were among the very few people she visited socially. She saw one other person, however. Charles Spencer Chaplin, the world's most famous comedian, occupied a substantial part of her time.

Chaplin's courtship of twenty-three-year-old Polita—the diminutive form by which she liked to refer to herself—was turbulent and easily as funny as Hollywood's best comedies. The comedian could be romantic, passionate, gallant. On one occasion he dashed out of a café on Hollywood Boulevard, bought a whole washbasket full of violets, and threw them at his heroine's feet. At other times he could be seen barreling down the street in her block-long limousine, kissing her hand at every turn of the wheel.

As early as November, 1922, the *Los Angeles Times* published a report on the pair and headlined it "The Queen of Tragedy to Wed the King of Comedy." While Polita exclaimed "This is the great love of my life," things were not yet so firmly settled. A later interview with Chaplin drew forth a diplomatic statement: "I cannot say yes. Any such answer must of necessity come from her. Neither can I say no. Think of the position that would place her in. She is a gentlewoman and a foreigner, don't you see? She doesn't understand American ways in affairs of this kind. She would resent my making a statement."

Polita certainly resented the statement that Chaplin made when the press pursued the matter. Apparently in a bantering mood, he mentioned to reporters that he could not marry until he completed his current picture. He added a generality on the order of, "A man must work. This is a workaday world, and we've all got to stay busy."

Reading this comment in the press, Pola saw in it a murderous onslaught against herself. What did the man mean? Was he saying she was too poor for him to marry? Was he making a crack about her desirability? He could not love her and say such a thing. Back and forth she paced, glaring at the tiger cub who was now her companion, and looking twice as ferocious. Weeping, stomping, invoking the gods. To work was unthinkable under these circumstances. She was ill. Seeck.

After three days of this torment, during which she refused to see Chaplin, Pola called reporters to her home and handed them a dignified little typewritten statement, which read as follows: "I consider that I am too poor to marry Charlie Chaplin. He needs to marry a wealthy woman, and he should have no difficulty finding one in the United States, the richest and most beautiful country in the world. Therefore I give Mr. Chaplin back his freedom and release him from his engagement. I wish him the best of luck, and I will always be his devoted friend."

In a trembling voice she added, "Three days I have thought I would do thees thing. I have not slept. Oh, it was a thousand little things. Oh, I don't know. It was just experience. A woman must learn by experience. I have not tell it to Mr. Chaplin to his face. I could not face that. I have sent my best friend to him. I will live only for my work. Happiness is over for me. The dear days at Del Monte and Santa Barbara, they can be no more."

The matter was far from over. A telegram arrived from Chaplin after she refused to see him. A return telegram went to his home. More telegrams followed. What she meant and what he meant. What she thought and what he thought. Denials, counter-denials, and counter-counter-denials.

Finally the beleaguered Pola gave in, and Chaplin dashed to her side. He had been only joking, he explained at her home in the early evening. His affection for her was complete and undying. Western Union messages had weakened Pola's resistance. Her lover's persuasive presence completed the process. At 10:30 P.M. the chef was given orders to serve a six-course dinner for two. Not until after midnight did the smiling Chaplin enter his limousine for the homeward journey.

"Pola gives Charlie the Air," the early night editions had said. The engagement was renewed in time for the late evening papers, and the following morning Pola confessed that she had been "too happy to sleep." Chaplin declared himself "the happiest man in the world." "Mr. Chaplin came to see me early, and he stayed late," she elaborated. "I have take him back, and we are quite reconciled and engaged again. He swore to me he never say he was too poor to marry me. He told me he love me and could not live without me. And so of course I believe him and have take him back."

While Pola was playing he-loves-me-he-loves-me-not with Chaplin, the film *Mad Love,* which she had made in Europe, was released in the United States by Goldwyn. The publicity gave the picture, a sort of *Camille* minus the cough, a royal send-off. Chaplin's simultaneous film, *A Woman of Paris,* also profited at the box office. The love affair, however, continued to see-saw.

Shortly after the reconciliation, when Pola went to visit the comedian in his home, a distraught young Mexican girl appeared from nowhere and started to attack her. Desperately in love with Chaplin, the girl had left her husband and traveled all the way from Mexico City to meet her screen idol. She had secretly entered the house, become unbalanced at the sight of Pola, and then attempted suicide. Similar incidents occurred later, for the gifted Chaplin tended to inspire extremely violent emotions in the opposite sex.

Pola could handle the competition, but she was not always sure she could handle Chaplin. There were the lovely idylls, weekends spent at Coronado, Santa Barbara, and at Pebble Beach. And there were the comedian's passionate declarations, his gallantries. But other factors too often pushed to the fore. Chaplin loved to talk at length about his own pictures, using his companion—often Pola—as a testing ground for ideas and effects. On the other hand, when Pola talked of her own filmmaking, Chaplin quickly grew distant. It was his world that he wanted to give Pola. He began building a house for the day when they would be married. All the plans were his own. When Pola, in an attempt to put at least one of her touches into the mansion, ordered a complete grove of tall trees transplanted to the grounds, Chaplin was thoroughly displeased. His jealousy, too, was constant and bothersome. Pola was not to dance with anyone else, not to smile too broadly at a man. Himself a virtual recluse, Chaplin's possessiveness kept Pola from fulfilling even necessary engagements.

As the year-end holidays of 1922 approached, Pola announced that she would give a Christmas Eve dinner to reunite all those people who had been kind to her in Hollywood. Chaplin curtly told her that he would be unable to attend because he would be working. On Christmas Day? This was really exaggerating, Pola felt. With considerable effort she convinced him that he should come.

All knew that the party would be a tacit celebration in honor of the lovers' engagement. Dinner was at seven; it was ten when Chaplin arrived. Calling her away from her guests, he handed her his engagement present, a large flawless pear-shaped diamond—lying unmounted in a jewel box. The busy lover apologized by saying he had not had time to have it set. For Pola, who would have liked to show off a tangible proof of her engagement, the dinner party was not an unmixed success. As the days went on, Chaplin kept looking at her hand for his stone. Explained Polita, "When I, too, have time enough, I shall have it mounted."

The affair came to a head when *Bella Donna* was finished. Pola was not looking forward to the première. She knew that her involvement with Chaplin had taken too much of her time, too much of the psychic energy she needed for her work. When Chaplin said he did not want her to go to the premiere but to spend the evening alone with him, a violent quarrel ensued. Pola missed the première. The press was quizzical, and Pola satisfied them.

"It end—like that!" she said, snapping her fingers. "I am very extreme. It is terrible. It was a most unhappy affair. The truth has not been told. It was not the mad love that the newspapers say. Not at all. Charlie appealed to my mother complex. And his personality interested me. I study. I study. And then I study too much. Always I have sought love. And always there have been disappointments. So now I am cynical. I am a fatalist. I believe in my star. It is my fate to be unhappy in love. I realized five weeks ago that it was an impossibility. Charlie is lacking in all matrimonial requirements. He is too temperamental. I'm glad it's over. Now I can think of my work again."

Foreswearing male company, Pola appeared happier after the breakup, spending a good deal of time with Kathlyn Williams, wife of the studio manager, Charles Eyton. Since she was obviously not going to move into Chaplin's house, she decided to buy her own. As usual, she did things on the grand scale, moving into the beautiful and wealthy Beverly Hills section. Her choice of house was American colonial, a $250,000 replica of Mount Vernon, the home of George Washington. Here she indulged her taste for good living. Yellow damask covered the walls, and rich white rugs decorated the floors. Venetian furniture of pale yellow with inlaid gold was ordered, along with prize oil paintings and first editions in five languages. Elaborate landscaping gave form to the palatial gardens and grounds.

Lavish parties became the order of the day, and with a retinue of servants that included a secretary, personal maid, cook, housemaid, gardeners, and a chauffeur, all ran smoothly—most of the time. There were notable exceptions. On one occasion either the servants made a mistake or an extra guest turned up. In any event, at the last minute the larder was short one wild duck, and Pola herself went down to the Beverly Hills butcher shop to get one. Just as the butcher was telling her he had no more, Pola's sharp eyes lighted on a bird. "But zat he iss a dawk," she said. The shop owner explained that it belonged to an aristocratic woman standing by the counter. To this woman Pola explained her predicament, but the lady was adamant. Pola gave a second, more emotional account of her need for the bird, but unfortunately her English ran out as she was reaching a melodramatic climax. The lady remained unmoved. Pola now slipped frenziedly into French, which the woman could not comprehend, and then into Russian, of which she understood even less. "No," was the only word that came from the lady's lips, for though the languages evaded her she sensed clearly enough that Pola was after her wild duck. In desperation Pola switched to her native Polish. At the door the elderly lady finally turned around in exasperation and hissed, "No, damn it! You can't have my duck." She then beat a hasty retreat before Pola could launch a new assault.

On another occasion the tranquillity of the Negri household was upset by a burglar who made the mistake of calling on her. Beverly Hills residents long remembered the night that began when the star was roused from her sleep by a series of strange sounds. It dawned on her that a burglar might be after the new chinchilla coat she had just purchased. Leaping from under the covers, Pola grabbed a trusty sixshooter, which she kept on hand for emergencies. Not too sure of what her next move should be, by way of compromise she aimed a couple of shots through the ceiling and waited. As mumblings from below came to her ears, she hurried to the window and poured a load of buckshot into the night air of the exclusive residential section; then she proceeded to alternate deep yells of "Help, help" with further discharges from her noisy weapon. The burglar obviously gave up on the chinchilla coat and fled. Indeed, it would not be surprising if the barrage of artillery fire had caused him to change professions.

Although Chaplin was no longer around to battle with her, Pola easily managed on her own to safeguard her reputation for being temperamental. One day she ordered the floors of her studio dressing room to be strewn with orchid petals, but unfortunately they gave her hay fever and had to be removed.

Another time a valuable brooch was missing, and a good bit of the lot was disassembled under the star's watchful eye while a search was made. Thereafter, Pola furnished her own private detectives to protect the jewels from her own collection that she wore during filming. Requests by the studio that she ship out on location were met by her insistence that they build the required set in Hollywood and save her the location trip. Even Laguna was too far for Pola, who found the phrase "I am very seeck" remarkably effective in making her points clear.

On a rainy day newspaper reporters could usually count on interesting copy issuing from a visit to Pola. When a reporter asked her what was the dangerous age for a man and a woman, she replied, "I do not know the dangerous age of man. I have not been one. The dangerous age of a woman is from one to a hundred." On another occasion she was asked to name the people in Hollywood she felt could really act. Pola came up with only six names. The outcry was deafening as the outraged egos of those omitted—most of Hollywood's stars—counter-attacked with lists of their own.

On the filmmaking scene, Pola's reputation for temperament continued unabated. She had had misgivings about *Bella Donna*, both because of her preoccupation at the time with Chaplin and also because the vampire role she played had been softened to make her character more sympathetic. Nevertheless, critics applauded her performance as brilliant and forceful.

This praise gave her added ballast when she was forced to sail into battle over her next film. *The Cheat* was the familiar story of a beautiful young wife sorely tempted out of the straight, narrow path of virtue by her craving for diamonds and ermine. George Fitzmaurice was again the director, which suited Pola well enough. What she didn't like was the screenplay, which had her jumping from an airplane into the water, from the water onto a motorcycle, from the cycle onto a moving train, with a chase along the roofs of the coaches as a clincher. Only after Pola tore a sizable hole in the roof were these acrobatics removed from the script.

"It's all so complex over here," she moaned after winning her battle. "You must think of exhibitors, of the Eastern office, of the censors, and of the public. In Europe we were free. We thought of nothing but our work. We did not even have to think of the public because we knew the public likes us and would be interested in any work into which we had put our hearts. Here you become so tired arguing, arguing, arguing, that you almost give up."

To Herbert Howe, Pola confided. "Ah, I have much trouble since I see you in Berlin. I suffer much. Yaas, I laugh there, but not here." The dashing Pola, with her aura for adventure, could get tired, but give up? Never. The humdrum, the domestic, the everyday ceased to exist when the alluring star made her appearance, and although Hollywood might be temporarily upset by her tantrums, forgiveness was inevitable when she paraded down Sunset Boulevard with a tiger on a leash, her sandaled feet exposing immaculately groomed toenails painted a fiery crimson.

From time to time, of course, Pola found it useful and even necessary to remind the former shopgirls, cowpokes, and plumbers' assistants who had become reigning screen stars that she, Pola, came from no such a workaday world. Pola Negri was in fact a bona fide countess, the Countess Domski, and her life prior to storming Hollywood had had more fireworks than a Cecil B. DeMille spectacle.

To begin with, there was this Hungarian gypsy father who had had the most profound influence on her—although he died when she was seven. As Pola told it, they used to sit around the campfire outside of Bromberg, Poland—where she was born in 1898 to the name of Apollonia Chalupec—and sing gypsy songs. Then her father would look into her eyes and make prophecies, most of them gloomy forecasts of upcoming disasters in the love arena.

Her mother had forbears who were of the Polish aristocracy, and Pola respected her stern, determined nature. But it was her father she adored. "My God, how handsome he was," she reminisced. "I look just like him." In 1905 the father joined the abortive Polish revolution. Pola hid under the bed when Russian

Cossacks came to the house to take him away to Siberia, from which he never returned.

With her mother and a younger brother she moved to Warsaw. Relatives helped to send her to an exclusive school run by the Countess Planten, and here she developed a great affection for the works of Italian poetess Ada Negri. Her favorite lines were revealing:

> *My thought, my will, my own;*
> *The brow that ne'er was bowed says:*
> *"I was born for laurel wreath and throne."*

High-strung and a rather bad student, Pola was next sent to the Imperial Ballet School, in St. Petersburg. But the strenuous régime and harsh climate brought on ill health, and she returned to Warsaw. Not, however, without a glowing memory. The Czar had come to visit the school and had been impressed by her beauty as it expressed itself in the performance of a barefoot Oriental dance. A chain encrusted with diamonds duly arrived from Nicholas I.

When she returned to Warsaw, the young girl learned with horror that her brother had died of the bubonic plague and that her mother was almost out of her mind with grief. Helping where she could at home, Apollonia found time to enter drama school, completing her course with honors and making her professional debut at the Kleines Theatre in Hauptman's *Hannele*. For the stage the fiercely patriotic Apollonia adopted the first four letters of her country's name, Pola, and the last name of her favorite poetess, Ada Negri. As Pola Negri she was highly acclaimed at the Kleines Theatre; then she was given a contract at a much higher salary to play the Imperial Theatre. Here the production of *Sumurun*, the fantasy in which she played the Slave of Fatal Enchantment, brought her tremendous favor.

When Pola chanced to see an American cowboy film, she was entranced by the new medium. Since there was no technical equipment available in Warsaw, she rented a photographer's studio and a camera, wrote a screenplay, and directed herself in the production of it. The film, *Love and Passion,* displeased her, and she sold it for a few rubles to a distributor who proceeded to make a fortune from it. The modest effort established her as her nation's film pioneer.

Success for Pola seemed always to be dulled by grief. A young painter came to do her portrait, and the two fell in love. They were planning their marriage when the young man fell ill of tuberculosis and died in her arms one bleak winter night. Her gypsy father's prophecy was already fulfilling itself.

There was nothing to do but work. And work was difficult with the Russians, the Germans, and the Poles all battling over the capital city. Before near-empty houses Pola played her Arabian Nights fantasy to the sound of exploding shells. And most disturbing of all, a suitor was sending her bouquets of white lilies and tuberoses nightly. It was maddening. Didn't the man know that in the gypsy lexicon white tuberoses spelled tragedy?

One night when Pola had just about had it, the cursed flowers arrived again. In a panic she rushed out of the theater to a little Bohemian café, where she ordered a glass of wine to calm her nerves. There was to be no relaxation, however. A man was staring at her, and though he did not interest her romantically, his face and eyes had a strength that fascinated her. Finally, he came and asked to sit with her. She recognized him. It was V.I. Lenin, the great revolutionary leader. Declaring that she was young and beautiful and he was growing old, the Marxist gave her the fruit of his lifetime of struggle—she should stick to her ideals, to whatever she believed in.

After an hour of sharing thoughts and philosophies, the two parted. Pola remembered his words, but she could not follow his advice. On returning to the theater, she found her mother waiting with the man who had sent the nightly flowers. He was Count Eugene Domski, scion of an aristocratic landowning Polish family. He had asked Pola's mother for her hand, and it had been granted. She and the Count exchanged formalities, and he left. Pola pleaded with her mother, but the latter was firm. She had made great sacrifices for Pola, and now here was an opportunity for a good match. White tuberoses or no white tuberoses, she would be married.

Ten days later the wedding knot was formally tied, and an apprehensive Pola was swept off to Count Domski's castle at Sassnowiece. The marriage was not a success. Domski was too cold and reserved for his volatile actress wife. He insisted that she give up her work and remain at his side. He also wanted an heir. For Pola the days and nights became increasingly lonely. She recalled that the great German director Max Reinhardt had seen her perform in Warsaw and had asked her to come to Berlin. Suddenly, without wasting another moment, Pola flew out of the gloomy castle and flagged a midnight train for Berlin.

Reinhardt welcomed her with open arms. Early in 1917 he produced the stage success *Sumurun*, which led to her fabulously successful film career with UFA. At the same time a prominent German businessman courted her and won her heart. When this came to the ears of Count Domski, he promptly entrained for Berlin and challenged the man to a duel. Panicky, Pola swore to the stars that she would give up her lover if he were spared. Miraculously the duel was in fact called off, and Pola gave up her heart's desire. She also gave up Domski, securing a divorce but judiciously retaining her title. In Berlin she was known both as Pola Negri, famous actress, and as Countess Domski.

While the Germans were fascinated with their imported Pole, they came to resent the fact that she was sending huge sums of money to support the war orphans of her native country. The fact that she also gave to German charities did not seem to help matters. As a result of this contretemps, Pola was doubly delighted when Adolph Zukor sent for her. "I am no more countess," she declared. "I am going to America." And when asked why she loved America so much, she replied candidly, "Because America loves me."

Events, moreover, proved that she was right. While some in Hollywood felt that she was haughty and snobbish, the flamboyant film capital basically approved of her antics. Her beauty, her exotic background, and her unorthodox behavior made for endless cocktail conversation.

Not only did Pola live as much as she possibly could, but sometimes it appeared as though she had lived through certain situations twice. Her memory of past affairs of the heart wavered with her mood. Of her meeting with Chaplin in Berlin she could say at one point, "The current of attraction ran between us and was unmistakable in its meaning to me. . . . The vibration between us was so tremendous that I began to be afraid." Once the romance was over, Pola remembered it differently. "Our association in Berlin, far from being romantic, was quite casual. I admired him as a personality and as an artist."

Pola began to enjoy the company of actor Rod LaRoque and tennis star Bill Tilden. The most flaming romance of her Hollywood days would soon begin. Meanwhile, she was making films, for which Paramount was paying her at the rate of half a million dollars a year.

In addition to *Bella Donna* and *The Cheat*, which also featured Jack Holt and Charles De Rochefort, the year 1923 saw Pola star in *The Spanish Dancer*, which was directed by Herbert Brenon and co-starred Antonio Moreno and Wallace Beery. In the same year Mary Pickford made the same story under the title of *Rosita*. Both efforts were considered artificial and tedious, though the heroines' performances were acclaimed.

In 1924 Herbert Brenon again directed her in *Shadows of Paris*, with Charles De Rochefort and Adolphe Menjou. Two films with la Negri were part of the studio directors' tour of duty at this time, but no more than two.

In order to please Polita her old favorite, Ernst Lubitsch, was brought in to direct *Forbidden Paradise*, with Menjou and Rod LaRoque. Speaking in German, the star and her director got along well, despite occasional spats. "Drehen," Lubitsch would order, and the cameras would whirr when tempers rose.

One of the last scenes showed Pola, as a Czarina, and LaRoque, as a young army officer of her court, in a passionate love scene. As Pola flung her arms about LaRoque's neck

Lubitsch slyly said, "Now Pola, now all the fervor of love—as though you really felt it." Pola looked at her director with a funny little smile and answered in German, "Ah, my dear Ernst, do not worry. I feel it all right."

Moments later Lubitsch stopped the cameras. "But his face powder has all come off on your cheek," he told Pola. "Can I help it?" she cried. "Yes, but even in the fervor of love, you keep your face between me and the camera so they can't see poor Rod at all," LaRoque wailed. While Lubitsch smiled wryly, Pola screamed with laughter. The film was a distinct success, with Pola more lovely and better gowned than at any time since her arrival in the United States.

Having placated their star with Lubitsch, the studio now imported another of her former European directors, Dmitri Buchowetsky, to direct her in *Lily of the Dust*, with Noah Beery and Ben Lyon, and in *Men*. Buchowetsky, a thirty-year-old Russian, spoke even worse English than Pola. As his art director he chose a former officer of the German dragoons, while cast members included a Russian prince, several Frenchmen, and a Rumanian. In this tower of Babel leading man Robert Frazer could find no one to whom he could speak English. Pola and Buchowetsky had a grand time Berlitzing all over the lot, but unfortunately the films did not reflect their elated spirits.

Ready-made stories seemed to be threatening Pola Negri's distinctive style. To the rescue in 1925 came novelist Joseph Hergesheimer with an original screenplay about a high-born lady. Entitled *Flower of the Night*, the film was directed by Paul Bern and co-starred one Yucca Trubetzkoy. Other 1925 efforts included *East of Suez*, directed by Raoul Walsh, with Edmund Lowe and Noah Beery, Sr.; *The Charmer*, directed by Sidney Olcott, with Robert Frazer; and *A Woman of the World*, directed by Malcolm St. Clair, with Holmes Herbert. Definitely not for children, *A Woman of the World* had Pola playing a dangerous, cynical, tempestuous Italian countess who wore a tattoo, the insignia of an amorous adventure.

The pace of filmmaking was grueling for Pola, who in Europe

had become accustomed to long, leisurely vacations between pictures. Here in America there was hardly enough time for pleasure, for romance, for feuds, such as the famous one that pitted Pola against the studio's other top female star, Gloria Swanson.

Queen Gloria was already reigning at Paramount when Pola made her celebrated entrance on the American scene, in late 1922. Moreover, Gloria had been there a long time, having made her film debut in her native Chicago in 1913 at the age of fifteen. When her aunt had taken her to the pioneer Essanay studio to watch the funny people making movies, a director had asked her to hand a bridal bouquet to leading lady Gerta Holmes—in those early days filmmaking was quite as casual as that. Rushes of the brief scene revealed a remarkably photogenic young Gloria, who was put on as a guaranteed extra at $13.25 a week. "I was far more excited about a bigger event in my life," Gloria later recalled. "I had just been kissed by a boy wearing an orange tie, and I was sure I was going to have a baby."

Gloria didn't have a baby, but she went on to bigger and better roles, graduating to Mack Sennett comedies. In only one, her last for the slapstick producer, did she wear a bathing suit. Nonetheless she was thereafter referred to as a former Mack Sennett "Bathing Beauty." "I want to wring people's hearts and cry and die all over the place," she had told Sennett, who proceeded to tear up her contract.

To many, Gloria's pretensions must have seemed ludicrous. The cameras thought otherwise. Gloria was short, not quite five feet tall, but she didn't look small. Her retroussé nose appeared elegant, her large mouth seductive, her big eyes luminous. She had large shoulders, but a clever clothes sense hid their true proportions.

Good starring roles for Triangle caught the eye of Cecil B. DeMille, who saw that Gloria could display enormous poise and grace. DeMille proceeded to cast her in the role of the rich society woman who was a cross between a vampire and a leading lady. He gave her all the trappings of the vamp—bizarre coiffures, fantastic headdresses, long, slinky, elegant gowns, and resplendent jewelry—but the characterizations were essentially sympathetic. Gloria designed many of the clothes herself and gave herself the appellation "Clotheshorse," which stuck. For two years DeMille put her through the paces in pictures such as *Male and Female, Why Change Your Wife?*, and *The Affairs of Anatel.*

After switching to Paramount in about 1922, Gloria began playing varied roles, including hoydenish schoolgirls and gauche waitresses, but the vamp image clung to her as a result of the DeMille period. The famous director had left her with another heritage. Striving for realism, he had used the real thing in his pictures—expensive jewelry, sable, ermine, and Mumm's champagne rather than a ginger ale substitute. Gloria had gotten used to good things and to the attention and acclaim that went with them.

When word came to her shell-like ears that Adolph Zukor had thrown one of Gotham's most fabulous parties for the new arrival, la Negri, la Swanson's reaction was brief but ear-splitting: "You can't do this to me!" Three weeks later Zukor hosted a splendid dinner for Gloria at New York's fashionable Park Lane Hotel, with French cuisine, served on the finest goldplate. The Negri liquor bill was matched dollar for dollar.

A spirited running battle between the two queens of the lot developed, helped along by press cheerleaders. Gloria soon learned of Pola's psychological warfare during filming, her late arrivals, tantrums, illnesses. One day, caught in the act of ducking off her own set, she was ready with a line borrowed from Pola: "Seeck, must go see doctor."

A clever old lady, adept at panhandling, turned the feud to her own advantage. When Polish people in need came to her asking for money, Pola was in the habit of telling her secretary, "Geeve him feefty dollars," whether the applicant was known to her or not. In this case the request came in the form of a letter, which the secretary read aloud. Pola was about to give her usual generous answer when she heard the postscript, which said, "I wrote to Gloria Swanson to ask for help, but she never answered my letter." "Hmmm, so Gloria sent her notings," Pola mused. "Well, I, Pola, will send her something. Send her two hundred dollars!"

Pola was swift to notice Gloria wheeling down Sunset Boulevard in her leopard-upholstered Lancia, with Wally Reid's robin's-egg blue town car not far behind and Mae Murray's canary Pierce-Arrow coming from the other direction. It was not long before Pola was careening about in her own custom-built limousine.

Lilyan Tashman had the seat of her toilet upholstered in genuine sable, but it was bathtubs which were one of the great Hollywood prestige symbols. Charles Ray, his head swelled by success in country bumpkin roles, ordered a cut-glass version from a New York jeweler at a reported cost of $75,000. Producer Mack Sennett had a two-ton tub hewn out of marble, decorated it with silver trimmings, and installed it in the tower office overlooking his studio. The objet d'art was eight feet long and five feet wide. Among the women, toilet splendor spelled Gloria Swanson, whose stunning golden bathtub was centered in a room of black marble. There was nothing for latecomer Pola Negri to do but to have a giant Roman plunge installed in her home.

The two enchantresses shared many of the same tastes. If Pola stocked her house with rare books and valuable paintings, Gloria's twenty-two room, cream-colored stucco mansion, situated on four acres in Beverly Hills, was equally magnificent. Priceless embroidered tapestries lined many walls, an enormous reception room was draped in peacock silk, a magnificent carved staircase led to huge rooms on the second floor, including one that housed a fully equipped motion picture theater.

Never trivial, Gloria maintained other establishments besides the Beverly Hills home—a country place at Croton-on-the-Hudson, a New York apartment, and a place in Paris. Pola took on no New York properties, but she did purchase the forty-two room Chateau Rueil de Seraincourt in Normandy. Busts of two Roman emperors graced the entrance, and tall black cypress trees lined a dark lagoon populated by swans and surrounded by graceful fountains. A private chapel was situated in the middle of a lovely myrtle grove. Animals on the Louis XIII showplace were named for friends, one duck bearing the appellation "Chaplin" because Pola thought it walked like the comedian.

When traveling, Queen Gloria engaged country estates and entire floors of hotels for her entourage of secretaries, friends and their relatives, handmaidens, and bushbeaters. Like Pola, she could be extremely generous with those she liked. On one occasion, at a dinner for three hundred people, she gave favors of solid gold compacts to all the women present and solid gold cigarette cases to all the men. Like Pola, she had a flair for the flamboyant. Ducking into Cartier's to escape a mob of well-wishing fans, she emerged with a pair of jewel-encrusted crystal bracelets that cost more than $20,000. To a reporter she once admitted that she could not remember within $50,000 how much she had been paid for making a certain film.

In the matter of men, both women were inordinately fond of their fathers. "I had no brothers or sisters, and father lavished upon me all the companionship he would have given a son," Gloria told a reporter. "There were long walks with him and long talks." Like Pola's father, Gloria's had given her advice: "There isn't an experience in the world that can't do you some good."

Gloria could match Pola's early marriage to Count Domski with her own wedlock at seventeen to actor Wallace Beery. They had divorced in 1919. Her romance with curly-haired Irish director Marshall Neilan was as turbulent as some of Pola's romances. After one argument she bopped him over the head with a magnum of champagne. "Any woman might, if you annoyed her enough, hit you over the head," Neilan commented philosophically. "Only with Swanson could you be sure it would be champagne, and a magnum at that."

An unhappy love for actor Herbert Marshall was broken off, and Gloria's second marriage was to Herbert Somborn, film producer and founder of Hollywood's famous Brown Derby restaurants. The couple divorced in 1923; custody of their daughter, as well as an adopted child, went to Gloria.

Gloria's third marriage was the sensation of 1925 in the film capital, and it clearly put her more than one up on Pola Negri. In Paris to film the comedy *Madame sans Gene*, which Pola had wanted to do, Gloria was delighted with a suave young man who was assigned by the studio as her interpreter. They got along so well that the young man began dating her. By the time the film was finished, they were engaged to be married. To old beau Marshall Neilan, Gloria wired, "Forget me." Neilan promptly wired back, "Forgotten." The man was no less than the Marquis Henri de la Falaise de la Coudraye, member of one of France's best families. He could trace his ancestry back in a direct line to 1190; he was handsome, cultivated, and a decorated war hero.

Pola's entry to America in 1922 had been dazzling. In 1925 Gloria's return was still more glittering. New York welcomed her with a tickertape parade, but it was Hollywood that pulled out all the stops. At the railroad station the diminutive star and her titled escort were met by city officials, brass bands, mountains of flowers, and banners that said "Welcome Gloria." Long lines of limousines fought their way through a sea of humanity as the parade wound its way to the Paramount studio, every inch of window space in office buildings enroute crowded with faces straining to catch a glimpse of Gloria Swanson, the former notions counter clerk from Chicago who had made good.

That evening frantic police fought to control the crowds outside the theater where *Madame sans Gene* was having its première. Inside, a distinguished, elegantly dressed audience sat in eager anticipation, the flags of France and the United States side by side near the screen, a symphony orchestra playing an overture. When a small, hesitant figure wrapped from head to toe in shimmering silver lamé came slowly down the aisle, the orchestra began playing "Home Sweet Home." The usually hard-boiled Hollywood audience rose to its feet to cheer. Gloria Swanson had come home.

She had come home, moreover, with a delightful comedy

triumph. *Madame sans Gene* was the tale of a sharp-tongued laundress who became a duchess, defied Napoleon, and saved his empress from disgrace. The role had been played on stage by Rejane and Ellen Terry, but the updated film version did not suffer by comparison.

For Gloria all was glorious. There were three lavish dinner parties tossed by Paramount, a star-studded soirée given by her old mentor, Mack Sennett, and best of all there was her handsome marquis husband. Liveried footmen were installed in their new household, and the invitations that went out began, "Madame la Marquise wishes to invite. . . ."

For the Countess Domski it was all too much. She fumed, beat on doors, strode on carpets, and issued assorted noises until Paramount gave her a glittering and costly party, although she had married no one and had not been away. "There is no rivalry," Pola declared when asked about the alleged feud. "She is clever. But it has always been my policy to be first wherever I am." The statement summed up the relationship with great accuracy. The dual queens actually liked and respected one another. It was just that each felt obliged to protect her position. They managed this simply by getting up in the morning.

Gloria soon dropped the aura of nobility and began calling her husband "Hank." Before long she also dropped Hank, going on to three additional marriages, all failures. She rejected a Paramount contract that gave her one million dollars a year and turned to independent production. She lost a fortune and made another with the guidance and help of Joseph P. Kennedy. Halfway measures were never tailored to the grandeur of Gloria Swanson, who returned to a spectacular screen triumph in *Sunset Boulevard* in 1950. Playing an aging, washed-up movie queen, she uttered the memorable lines: "I'm still big. It's the pictures that have gotten smaller." For Gloria the lush days were never really over. Sometime after the film's première she appeared on a television show and dropped her coat. When a gallant gentleman stooped to pick it up, Gloria stopped him. "Never mind," she said, "it's only last year's mink."

It was the sort of grand gesture that would have appealed to

Pola Negri, past mistress of grand gestures. While Gloria was turning into royalty back in 1925, little Polita was embarked on a headline-splattering affair of her own. She was in love with the screen's greatest lover, Rudolph Valentino, the Sheik.

Rudy, only a bit player at the time, had sent her a fan letter at the height of her European success, but in the years that she had been in Hollywood they had never met. His vertiginous success as a romantic idol had not escaped her notice, however, nor had his extraordinary good looks—the dark eyes set wide apart, unfathomable beneath heavy black brows, the full, sensitive lips, a classic aquiline nose, the sleek face, vibrant with life and yet betraying a hint of disillusion.

Pola's mother had joined her in Hollywood, and one day she told her daughter that she had heard Valentino wanted to meet her. There was a party the following Sunday to which both were invited. For the occasion Pola dressed all in white—snow-white Russian kid boots, a white dress, a white fox fur tossed over her shoulder. In solitude and silence she sat in a chair by a large bay window—waiting as if for her destiny to be fulfilled. To her extreme annoyance, Valentino never showed up.

The meeting of the two was only briefly delayed. Several nights later at a resplendent costume ball given by Marion Davies, Pola appeared in the Czarina costume she had worn in *Forbidden Paradise.* Valentino arrived in the toreador costume from his film *Blood and Sand.* He bowed low, took her bejeweled hand, and kissed it. He invited her to dance. The two moved easily, responsive to each other's slightest prompting, the cynosure of all eyes even in these glamorous surroundings.

The romance that developed between them was as complex as the two temperaments involved. Rudy was attracted to Pola's midnight beauty, to her sharp wit, her keen love of life. She loved his gentleness, his sincerity, his confiding nature.

But then at times everything came apart at the seams. A misunderstanding would bring Valentino charging over to the Negri residence, where on one occasion he kicked in the plate glass window of the living room. Or perhaps a third person would appear on the scene, and tempers would flare, Slav vying with Latin. Rudy's gorgeous solitaire would vanish from Pola's hand. Then notes would pass back and forth. Appeals. Apologies. Reconciliations. Talk of a secret wedding would alternate with rumors of a complete breakup. "From day to day you cannot tell whether they are engaged in a none too private affair or whether they are engaged in a none too private war," wrote one observer.

When Rudy went to Paris to secure a divorce from his second wife, Natacha Rambova, many were surprised at the length of his stay. But when he returned his arms were full of expensive gifts for his Pola.

In the late spring of 1926 they were separated again, when Valentino was ordered to New York for personal appearances to publicize his latest film, *Son of the Sheik.* Pola went to the railroad station to see him off, again and again telling his manager, George Ullman, to bring him back to her soon. "Oh, Rudy, I am sad, sad," she said, and waved goodbye as the train pulled out.

Valentino did not come back to her. In mid August he developed severe stomach pains and was carried into Polyclinic Hospital in New York. What was first presumed to be appendicitis turned out to be a perforated ulcer. A double operation for appendicitis and gastric ulcers was an apparent success, but a short time later he developed local peritonitis. "Valentino Chances for Recovery Thought Slim," read the headlines. Hour by hour the public and the papers waited for reports from the hospital. Good news and bad alternated. In Hollywood, Pola lived near the phone. The studio, eager to have her complete her current film, *Hotel Imperial,* tended to shrug off her fears, emphasizing each encouraging note in the medical reports.

Everything apparently hinged on how strongly Valentino's body could resist infection. He was only thirty-one, but he had lived at a perilous pace, had been too sensitive to criticism, too eager to live up to his image as a swashbuckling hero. From Paris, Natacha Rambova cabled that she was praying for his recovery. Jean Acker, his first wife, had previously made inquiries. Messages arrived from Chaplin, Marion Davies, Mae Marsh, and Mary Pickford. Gloria Swanson, in New York, telephoned, and United Artists board Chairman Joseph Schenck arrived with his wife, Norma Talmadge. Most persistent were the calls from Pola Negri in Hollywood.

On August 23, Rudolph Valentino took a sudden turn for the worse and died. On learning the news, Pola suffered a complete collapse and was placed under sedation. It was many hours before she regained her composure, but when she did, a firm decision had lodged itself in her mind: she would go to New York to be with the body. Word was sent ahead that she was coming, that the funeral must be postponed, that the coffin should remain open. Hastily attiring herself in black silk and a black cloche hat, Pola went to the railroad station accompanied by Marion Davies and several other friends, her doctor, a nurse, and a secretary. Paramount cooperated by sending along publicity representative Harry A. Klemfuss.

Aboard the Golden State Limited, Pola was in a state of prostration. The nurse made constant application of ice bags to her head and above her heart. No admission was granted to the narrow confines of her drawing room. At towns along the way crowds gathered to catch a glimpse of the grieving star; each time they were disappointed.

Reporters were similarly rebuffed, but enroute Pola dictated answers to written questions to her secretary, Florence Hein. When the Golden State Limited stopped at Chicago's LaSalle Street station to be switched onto the Twentieth-Century Limited for the five-day journey's final lap, these answers were handed to the press.

"My love for Mr. Valentino was the greatest love of my life; our souls met upon our lips; I shall never forget him," she began. "I loved the irresistible appeal of his charm—the wonderful enthusiasm of his mind and soul. I didn't realize how ill he was, or I would have been there before his death; he kept the seriousness of his illness from me."

The next statements produced headlines around the country. "Mr. Valentino proposed to me after he returned from Paris a free man. There was only one thought in our minds. We looked forward to the time when we could be together for eternity. Ours was the one great love of our existence. For both of us past affairs only proved and strengthened this belief. Before settling down to a life of perfect domestic happiness it was his wish as well as mine that we should make one picture together. This would have been the final picture of my career. Then would have come the children he loved so dearly.

"His love was the most devoted and unselfish love. The predominant trait of his character was his appreciation of all that was good and beautiful. His thoughtfulness of others. My last message from him came Saturday morning before his relapse. He was overjoyed at my coming to his bedside and sent me his devoted and sincere love. He could hardly wait for my coming."

As confirmation of their closeness, a radiogram was produced from Rudy's brother Albert. Addressed to Pola, it read: "Only you and I can realize this loss."

Many skeptics doubted Pola's word of her engagement to be married to the Sheik. Statements were recalled in which he had said he would not marry before his film career was over; others had heard him say that if he married again, it would be to a woman of his own Italian race who would bear him many children.

Some viewed Pola's grief as merely an elaborate publicity maneuver. "They do not understand me," Pola said in her own defense. "I am a child of my race. I am Slav. I cannot help that I have not the restraint of the Anglo-Saxon. My emotions seem to them exaggerated, but I am not acting."

Certainly Pola's manifestations of grief were no more extraordinary than those of the crowds who lined up to view Valentino's bier, at Campbell's Funeral Parlor at Broadway and 66th Street in New York. On Tuesday, August 24, more than 200 policemen tried to keep in check a queue that was estimated at more than 15,000 persons. In sullen file they moved slowly to the tune of a great organ in the parlor. When a downpour added its discomfort to the frustrations of the long

Pola Negri

Pola Negri arrived in New York City in 1922 before embarking for Hollywood and a career in American films.

Charlie Chaplin and "The Wildcat."

La Negri starred with Jack Holt in *The Cheat,* 1923, directed by George Fitzmaurice.

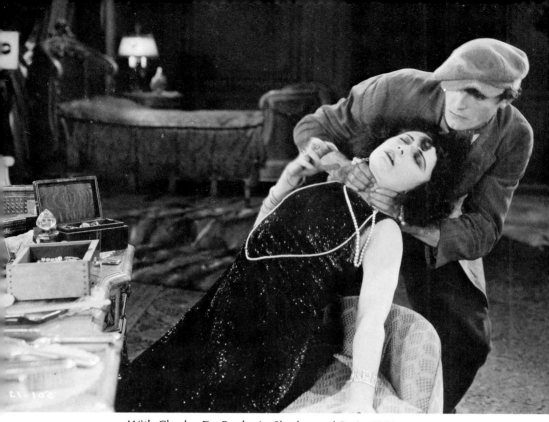

With Charles De Roche in *Shadows of Paris*, 1924.

Pola with director Dmitri Buchowetsky on the set of *Men*, 1924.

Robert Frazer played opposite Pola
in *Men*.

Pola as the jaded heroine in *Shadows of Paris*.

The emphasis was on "naughty" in Pola's performance of *Good and Naughty*, 1926, directed by Malcolm St. Clair.

The Shadows of Paris. Pola Negri's distinctive style and her offstage histrionics kept her in the public eye.

During the filming of *Hotel Imperial* (above) Pola agonized over the illness of her lover, Rudolph Valentino.

A scene from *Barbed Wire*, a 1927 Paramount production.

While Pola mourned over the death of Valentino, she worked harder than ever. Gustav von Seyffertitz was a co-star in *Barbed Wire*, directed by Rowland Lee.

Are Women to Blame? was made in 1928. At this time the press was particularly hard on Pola, chiding her for finding a new love (Serge Mdivani) so soon after Valentino's death.

Pola poured out her heart during a 1928 radio tribute to the late Rudolph Valentino.

Nils Asther and Pola in *Loves of an Actress,* a 1928 production.

Gary Cooper escorts Pola to a Hollywood party.

In *Hi Diddle Diddle* Pola's comedy role lampooned the temperamental Negri of the hectic days of the vamps. With her are (left to right): Billie Burke, Adolphe Menjou, and June Havoc.

Pola Negri returned to pictures in *The Moonspinners* (1963), starring Hayley Mills.

lines, a stampede began. Twice the mob rushed the parlor, pressing against a plate glass window, which broke, injuring dozens. Others clawed one another in the face, tearing off hats and clothing, screaming, fainting. Sixty police reserves were rushed to the scene to stop the city's worst riot in twenty years.

The following day thousands more lined up to view the coffin, half closed with the bronze, the other half beyond reach but showing through a thick plate of glass the screen idol's still handsome face. His body was dressed in formal evening attire. Three doctors and a nurse were in attendance in a room set aside for the purpose. The steady stream flowing past the casket had numbered well over 35,000 when disorder threatened once more, and George Ullman, dismayed by the lack of reverence displayed by the surging mob, ordered the coffin closed to public view at midnight. An honor guard of black-shirted Italian Fascists, which had stationed itself in the parlor, was also dismissed. It was known that Valentino had felt that he was badly treated on his last visit to Italy and that he was anti-Mussolini. Il Duce had sent no floral offering, and the honor guard was a local unit's manifestation of sympathy. One of the last to view the coffin before it was closed was Jean Acker, who said that she had just reconciled with Rudy, that they had always retained their love for each other, that her affection for him was of a motherly-sisterly nature.

On the morning of August 29, the Twentieth-Century Limited arrived at New York's Grand Central Station. Clad all in black, Pola was met by manager Ullman, and she maintained her composure until they reached the upper level. As the crowd moved forward and news cameras flashed, Pola gave a look of indignation and broke into hysterical weeping. "No, no," she said to cameramen and was led swiftly to a side exit and a limousine, which took her to the Hotel Ambassador.

In a hotel drawing room she met briefly with reporters. "The newspapers have been very cruel, but I suppose some of you understand," she said. For the press a letter was read which had been written to Pola by Harold Meeker, the doctor who had operated on Valentino. It described the dying Sheik's last moments and concluded with the words, "Pola—if she does not come in time, tell her I think of her." At this Pola uttered a cry and was hurried to another room by her nurse.

Crowds gathered once more when later in the day Pola went to the Campbell Funeral Parlor to view the bier, opened by special permission of the city's health department. Tears were streaming down her cheeks as she made her way unsteadily toward the casket. For long minutes she gazed at the face of the man she loved; then she fell to her knees and began softly intoning the lengthy 'Litany of the Dead.' As she said the final words, the strain became too great. Pola collapsed and fell unconscious. The Ullmans, who had accompanied her, ministered to her. Not until half an hour later were they able to call in the waiting press.

Columnist Whitney Bolton later described the scene that ensued. As eighteen news cameramen began shooting, Pola took directions from the photographers as though shooting a picture. "Okay, Pola, give us the bended-knee-in-grief bit," one shouted. "Now, Pola, lean over the coffin and give us some tears we can photograph," said another. Bolton heard one enterprising young man ask her to place a white rose on Valentino's chest. This photograph never appeared—obviously the photographer did not know the sinister place that the gypsy lexicon of evil omens assigns to the white rose. According to Bolton, Pola was at the funeral parlor for two hours, giving the cameramen every pose except the one with the rose.

At ten in the morning on August 30, for the first time in motion picture history the entire industry came to a standstill. For two minutes all heads were uncovered and bowed in memory to the dead star. "Rudolph Valentino's service to humanity was as great as that of any rabbi, priest, or clergyman," read a statement from Louis B. Mayer. Other tributes poured in from the great names of the film world.

At eleven o'clock a solemn high mass was to be celebrated over the body at St. Malachy's Roman Catholic church on West 49th Street, much frequented by actors. Again, tremendous crowds gathered as a three-car cortège followed the body from

Campbell's to the church. In the first car were the Campbell staff; Pola Negri, shrouded from view in a veil of heavy mourning, and the Ullmans were in the second; Jean Acker and her mother in the last. Sobbing and red-eyed, strikingly unlike the beautiful, dynamic actress known on the screen, Pola was led down the aisle to a front row seat, near her Norma and Constance Talmadge, Nora Van Horn, a half sister of Natacha Rambova, and the Ullmans. Her head bent, Pola was so close that she could have touched the coffin simply by reaching out.

Adolph Zukor, Marcus Loew, and Joseph Schenck were among the 500 friends who had been admitted to the church, although more than 10,000 had made requests. Gloria Swanson was there, along with Marilyn Miller, Hope Hampton, Harry Houdini, Major Edward Bowes, George Jessel, Lois Wilson, Madge Bellamy, Richard Dix, Mary Pickford, Douglas Fairbanks, Jean Acker, and many other well-known names. The ushers included Richard Dix, Ben Lyon, the Marquis de la Falaise de la Coudraye, Clifton Webb, and Kenneth McKenna.

With the Reverend Edward F. Leonard in attendance, Guido Ciccolini of the Chicago Opera sang the miserere mass. Dimitri Onotri of the San Carlo Company sang Gounod's "Ave Maria." Floral tributes were piled high around the closed casket. A $2,000 offering by Pola had been rejected as too large and conspicuous. Pola ordered it destroyed. She substituted a smaller carpet of red roses, which was placed on the casket. As it was borne down the main aisle at the end of the mass, sobs overcame the congregation. In her front pew Pola was near collapse. In the rear, nightclub entertainer Texas Guinan wept with two of her girls, one of them dancer Ruby Keeler. A boyhood friend of Valentino's threw himself over the passing coffin and had to be restrained, and two tabloid photographers, hidden in the choir loft, were forcibly ejected.

After the mass, the dead star's body was returned to the Gold Room on the third floor of Campbell's Funeral Church, there to await the arrival of his brother from Paris via the White Star steamship *Homerica.* "Her best performance," whispered Regina Cannon of the *New York American* as Pola left.

In the next day's papers Pola read with amazement that she had swooned and fallen into the arms of "Dr. Wyman." It turned out that the latter was a suave impersonator who had several times in the past insinuated himself into situations involving celebrities or prominent personalities. On one occasion he had attached himself to the suite of a prominent orthopedic surgeon, and another time he had been convicted of impersonating a navy officer at a reception tendered to Princess Fatima of Afghanistan when she visited the United States in 1923. He had also served a prison term after he had made misrepresentations in order to secure an interview with President Warren Harding.

Wyman had so thoroughly impressed George Ullman with his standing as a physician that he actually managed to take charge of the distribution of the official reports of Dr. Harold Meeker and other surgeons who detailed the illness of Valentino for public print. According to Ullman, he had displayed a police badge and rode in police cars. He convinced everyone that he was on the staff of Flower Hospital.

When the "doctor" went so far as to make an appearance at Pola Negri's suite at the Ambassador, the subdued star of the silver screen found some of her old vigor. "I did not faint in any doctor's arms," she cried. "Let me get at that imposter." For some time the efforts of her nurse, the secretary, and other attendants in the suite were required to calm the storm. Hearing the screams, Wyman disappeared down the corridor.

On Wednesday, Pola went to the pier to meet Alberto Guglielmi, the brother of Rudy. The crush to see the encounter was so great that customs inspectors found it difficult to handle the baggage. Still the picture of grief and sorrow, Pola embraced her dead love's brother. Alberto, three years older than Rudy, spoke of Pola as "the woman my brother loved so dearly and whose marriage I had hoped would soon be a living reality."

Because of Valentino's divorce a special dispensation was needed to bury him in Hollywood Cemetery. With his body, Pola, brother Alberto, and the Ullmans left Grand Central on September 2 and headed for the West Coast. For the press Pola had a statement: "On the eve of my departure for California I wish to take this opportunity to express my most sincere thanks to my many dear friends in New York who have offered me their sympathy in this dark hour of my sorrow. It is a great consolation to know that the last remains of my beloved will find a resting place in California, the spot where he rose to fame and spent so many hours in the home he loved so dearly."

It was almost two weeks after the Sheik's death, on September 6, 1926, that his body finally arrived in Los Angeles. Authorities feared a repeat of the New York disorders, so the casket was removed at a suburban point and taken from there to the funeral parlor. Marion Davies had boarded the train earlier in the day, and she accompanied her friend Pola, who left her stateroom as the train stopped at the little station. Weeping, Pola walked to the casket and placed a large wreath of yellow roses on it. In an extremely nervous condition she entered a limousine with Marion, her nurse, and a physician.

On September 7, Hollywood paid its last respects to the man who had captured the imagination of millions. A funeral procession extended for three miles through crowded streets, down Santa Monica Boulevard to Hollywood Cemetery. A requiem high mass was followed by simple services. June Mathis, the woman who had given Rudy his first big chance in *The Four Horsemen of the Apocalypse*, was there, as was Norman Kerry, the star's closest friend. Others present were Charlie Chaplin, Marion Davies, Ernst Lubitsch, Mabel Normand, Antonio Moreno, Estelle Taylor, Jack Gilbert, James Quirk (the publisher of *Photoplay*), the Ben Turpins, the Harold Lloyds, Cecil B. DeMille, Samuel Goldwyn, Jesse Lasky, William S. Hart, Louis B. Mayer, Hal Roach, Mack Sennett, Erich Von Stroheim, Marshall Neilan, Sid Grauman, and many more.

As in New York, the center of attention in the small chapel of the Church of the Good Shepherd in California was Pola Negri, garbed in black satin, veiled in crepe. Rosary in hand, her kneeling figure cast a poignant shadow in the small, candlelit chapel. Her cries and those of Alberto rose above the suppressed sobs of the others. After the service the casket was borne over a flower strewn path to a marble mausoleum just around the corner from the crypt of another famous star, the ill-fated Barbara LaMarr. Overhead an airplane dropped clusters of roses from the sky, a final token of love. The Hollywood ceremonies had been dignified; the only untoward incident was the ejection from the chapel of a girl, weeping convulsively, who had been hiding all night in hope of seeing the body of her idol.

The country's emotional binge was largely over. The Valentino will left one dollar to his second wife, Natacha Rambova, and divided the estate into equal thirds for an aunt of Natacha who had remained close to Rudy, for brother Alberto, and for a sister, Maria. Pola Negri was not mentioned in the will, which was dated September 1, 1925, a matter of days after Valentino first met Pola, at Marion Davies's masquerade. The document indicated that he had had premonitions of death, for it specified that should he die, the distribution of his last picture, *The Son of the Sheik*, should not be impeded. This later made a small fortune for the beneficiaries of the will. It also enabled the estate to pay back—at 7 percent interest—the $15,000 that Pola had loaned to Rudy.

In October, Pola announced that she would move into Falcon's Lair, Valentino's fabled mansion, built high on a peak to resemble a medieval castle, which he had furnished with priceless possessions. The terraced gardens, the aviary, the purple and gold bedroom, and the scarlet and black living room would be hers, Pola said. "Rudolph and I had planned to live there after our marriage, so I'm very happy to have it for myself." But plans went awry; within the year Falcon's Lair went under the hammer at public auction.

"Where am I? What am I? What is all this about?" Valentino had asked at the height of his kaleidoscopic fame. After his death there were as many questions about his relationship to Pola and even more varied answers. In his book about Valentino his manager, George Ullman, asked: "Were Pola Negri and Valentino engaged? I repeat that although I was entirely in his confidence, he never told me so, and I never asked him."

So extravagant had been the brouhaha surrounding

Valentino's death that many continued to feel that the Hollywood publicity machine must have been in operation. People came forward who said that on that first day when the body was put on public display, virtually no one braved the drizzly day to file into the funeral parlor. Paramount publicity representatives, it was said, paid dozens of pedestrians two dollars each to start the ball rolling. Seeing a line, others, like sheep, queued up, and finally a mob developed.

It is indeed possible that Paramount helped matters along, but the Valentino story had been in the headlines for weeks. The scenes that took place exploded out of a built-up ferment. Not only in New York but around the world the Valentino legend took hold, cults developed, young girls in distant countries committed suicide while embracing his autographed photo.

And for Pola Negri the fact that she was photographed in her moment of sorrow was not irreverent, nor was it bad taste to appear in beautiful black silk. On the contrary, for Pola it would have been gauche to appear in anything less than the best. She may have been personally bereft, but she was still the great screen actress, a public figure, and she never forgot it. For Polita's turbulent nature the supercharged emotionalism was merely par for the course.

When her physicians gave their approval, she went back to work. *Hotel Imperial* rolled off the assembly line. Swedish director Mauritz Stiller had made his first appearance on the lot stripped to the waist, a move to counter the heat. Pola retired to her dressing room until a shirt covered his torso. *The Crown of Lies* was directed by Dmitri Buchowetsky. Next, Malcolm St. Clair came in to direct a comedy, *Good and Naughty*, with Clive Brook. *Barbed Wire*, directed by Rowland V. Lee, also co-starred Brook. Stiller reappeared with his shirt on for *Woman on Trial*, with Einar Hansen and Lido Manetti.

Work helped Pola to regain her equilibrium. So did Russ Colombo, who had joined the three-piece orchestra that was now setting the mood for her filmmaking. Colombo's great dark eyes and sensitive features reminded Pola of Valentino. Still very young, he became a celebrated crooner, and he wrote songs dedicated to her. But tragedy intervened once more: Colombo accidentally shot himself while examining a Civil War cap and ball pistol. He was dead at twenty-six.

Pola continued her visits to Valentino's mausoleum, where she would go all in black to pray in a cold blue and purple light. The visits stopped shortly before May 14, 1927. On that date Pola married Prince Serge Mdivani at her chateau in Normandy.

"Whirlwind" certainly describes their courtship. The dark, handsome, debonair prince came from one of the best families of old Russia, his father having served as aide-de-camp to the late Czar. After the Communist revolution of 1917, the family had emigrated to Paris, and later several of the younger members came to America. With the family fortune gone, Serge had worked in the California oil fields, maintaining his ties, however, to many of the best houses. He had become the friend of Pola's mother, who invited him to visit her often.

In Pola, Serge saw at once a tempestuous beauty, a wealthy actress, and a woman made disconsolate by her lost love. He was affectionate and cavalier. For a time Pola resisted his attentions, but that was not easy. When she boarded a train for New York, she found that Serge had also bought a seat. When she booked passage on an ocean liner for Europe, a telephone call in the middle of the night revealed that the prince was on board. As his ardor increased, Pola's resistance weakened. An old friend gave last-minute advice. "Pola, please don't marry Serge Mdivani. It will be a tremendous mistake. I don't believe the marriage will work." Polita loved to receive advice, but she had a remarkable propensity for ignoring it. She married her prince.

Once more the press was hard on Pola, chiding her for finding a new love so swiftly after the demise of her beloved Valentino. Defenders were quick to point out that a cool, calculating woman would have had her romance in private. The candid, straightforward Pola wanted the world to know of her new romance, just as she had wanted it to see her earlier grief.

In Hollywood, Pola's contract was nearing its end. In 1928

she donned a blond wig to film *Three Sinners,* directed by
Rowland V. Lee and featuring Tullio Carminati and Paul Lukas.
Lee also directed *Secret Hour,* with Jean Hersholt, and *Loves of
an Actress,* with Nils Asther and Mary McAllister. *Are Women
to Blame?* was another 1928 entry. *Woman from Moscow* was
directed by Ludwig Berger, with Norman Kerry and Paul Lukas.
It was the last picture required by Pola's contract. With
considerable less fanfare than had attended her arrival, Pola left
for Europe with her prince.

"My life has been one revolution after another, and
Hollywood was the worst," she stated later, adding that it had
taken her favorite philosopher, Schopenhauer, to get her over
the worst parts of her stay. For Pola the climate was enervating,
the society lacking in stimulation, and the pace of
picture-making too fast and never entirely satisfactory.

Everyone agreed that something was wrong with Pola's
American films; they were popular, but they never reached the
heights of her earlier European productions. Blame was placed
on the directors, the stories, the tendency to make Pola appear
sympathetic even in roles that called for a more severe
characterization. "Damn sympathy," Pola shouted one day. "I
don't care whether they love me or not. I don't care whether I
am beautiful or not. I want a chance to act."

"I do not believe in star pictures," she said at another time.
"Each part should be played for its worth. I would rather have
less than my legitimate share so that people might go away
wishing they could have seen more of me." Whatever was
wrong, it was never corrected. An insidious process of
standardization undermined Pola's theory of acting and led to a
string of often mediocre pictures, which gradually sank to the
purely "program" type. The artistic capabilities of Pola Negri
were never really exploited in Hollywood.

Serge Mdivani was delighted when his wife embarked with
him for Europe. His courtly manner had gradually become more
domineering. He wanted her at his side, not delighting
anonymous thousands with her beauty and charm. Any curb on
her independence was a matter of concern to Pola, but a far

greater sadness now entered the couple's life: Pola became pregnant and lost her baby when she slipped and fell down the marble steps of an underground passage in the Normandy chateau.

Financial losses were added to other concerns as Pola sponsored her husband in different ventures. Grandiose entertaining and other manifestations of high living reduced the bankroll. The stock market crash of 1929 was the last and most powerful blow. Suddenly an estate of $5 million had largely evaporated.

In order to help recoup her fortune, Pola made a British film, *The Woman He Scorned*, directed by Paul Czinner. When a projected role in *The Queen's Necklace* called for her to bare her breasts for a red-hot iron, Serge became violently angry. Pola withdrew from the film, but the marriage did not have far to go. "Love must inspire me in my work, or it must go," Pola declared. "Love is disgusting when you no longer possess yourself." In 1931 she divorced the prince and announced that she was going back to work in Hollywood.

"I do not like the talkies," she had said when the new technique began sweeping the medium. "The motion picture should not try to imitate—try to replace—the stage. Bits of dialogue, perhaps in very tense scenes, are good. But people will tire of hearing those unreal voices from the screen. And the way they make talking pictures, it is very bad. They just let some one who can speak the lines have the parts. And in speaking they lose all those little artistic details and all the little subtleties of atmosphere that make the screen a really individual art."

Like many another star who had scorned sound pictures, Pola came back to give the talkies a whirl. *A Woman Commands* was filmed in 1932, the true story of Maria Draga of Serbia, a young commoner singing in a café, who attracted the love of the king. Although she was in love with another, he married her. The lover started a revolution, and before she could stop it, both she and the king were killed.

Pola's contract for the film stipulated that, as before, she could choose her own leading man and her director, and she could supervise her costumes. For the lover she settled on a young English actor named Laurence Olivier. When Olivier was stricken with jaundice, Basil Rathbone took his place. Roland Young played the king, and Paul Stein directed.

"Pola Negri's voice records perfectly and is as fascinating as her personality," said one critic when the film was released. Her heavy accent and the turgid story line did not meet with public approval, however, and no further Hollywood offers came Pola's way. A stage venture, *A Trip to Pressburg*, closed in Pittsburgh.

Bad health plagued Pola during the following months, and at one time she was reported in critical condition when a bad appendix demanded an emergency operation. Five different nationalities gave blood transfusions, and Pola quipped that she was now truly an international star.

When she had recovered, she began to throw extravagant beach parties at her Santa Monica home. Old and new friends came and producers, directors, and stars. But no film offers were forthcoming.

Pola took another look at Falcon's Lair, the old Valentino home, and decided that she would buy it. "I have definitely decided to make my home here for the rest of my life," she said. "And that is the only house I want. There I can live with my memories of our great love. I think Rudy would have it that way, too. He wouldn't want strangers in the house. . . . To strangers the home would merely have been a house. To me it is a shrine. I will ask for no other privilege than to spend the rest of my life in an atmosphere hallowed by the spirit of the man I loved so much."

The words had barely left Polita's lips before she packed her bags for Europe, a lucrative contract in her pocket for a series of films on the continent. Once again her incredible star was rising. In France she made *Fanatisme* in 1934; in Austria she filmed *Mazurka* in 1935. In the next years she made a number of films in Germany, including a highly praised version of *Madame Bovary*. In French and in German, Pola spoke fluently and without accent; only English brought out this handicap. Their success on the continent notwithstanding, these European films received scant attention in the United States, and for a time la Negri seemed to be forgotten. When her name again hit the front pages in America, it was with a typically sensational clap of thunder: Pola was rumored to be the mistress of Hitler!

"Everybody is talking in whispers of the course of Hitler's romance with the Polish film actress," said the *New York Post.* "The actress has been seen often in the dictator's company during the last few weeks, and it was noticed that he paid marked attention to her at the informal parties they attended together. Pola Negri recently said she was very much in love with an important person in Germany. 'I can say no more than that he is a very, very famous person.' she is reported to have said."

Both French and British newspapers later published articles that hinted that Pola had fallen out of favor with Hitler and had been put in a concentration camp. In response to this Pola brought suit and said: "I have never met Der Führer, and so a friendship with him was invented purely as a sensational news scoop. As I never mix in politics and have never been interested in them in the least, I would hardly be eligible for a concentration camp."

While Pola had never met the German dictator, Adolf Hitler had apparently been very fond of Pola's films, including those made in Austria and France in 1934 and 1935. Somehow, however, her name had been placed on a proscribed list of Jewish actresses, presumably because anonymous letters to the propaganda ministry accused her of anti-German activities abroad. Pleas to Joseph Goebbels to have her name removed from the list failed. At this point Hitler himself entered the scene, dispatching a delegation of his slickest Gestapo agents to Poland, where they waded through genealogical charts and came up with altogether satisfactory proof that Pola Negri was an Aryan and fully qualified to appear in German films. Thereafter, it was not uncommon for the Führer to send emissaries to the UFA production offices asking that a print of Pola's latest film be sent to the Chancellory to be run in his private projection room before its release.

The final word on Pola's alleged romance with Hitler came in an interview with Agnes Grunstrom, who had been the star's wardrobe mistress during her years at Paramount. Miss Grunstrom declared that all the talk was pure nonsense. "Miss Negri was herself a dictator," she said. "She would not stand for taking orders from even Hitler. They could not get along ten minutes together unless Pola is very much changed. . . . Those stories about her temperament—they were not even half the truth. Today all the stars in Hollywood put together are not so temperamental." From one who had dodged Pola's flying bric-a-brac for years, and heard her gypsy oaths in five languages, the statement seemed definitive.

While there was no affair with Adolf, Pola's heart was not idle during the period of the thirties. Chicago multimillionaire Harold McCormick was reported on the verge of marriage with Pola just before her departure for Europe. The trip spelled the end of their relationship.

"No more Mdivanis. That was a nightmare," Pola told the *New York Times* in 1935, and she added that she would marry a middle-aged British gentleman before Christmas. His name, she said, must remain secret, for he was "a very famous statesman, a former member of Parliament, and enormously wealthy." "That is all I can tell you now because the elections are going on, and it might make things difficult," Pola explained. "He is about ten or fifteen years older than I am and tremendously intellectual—that's what I want now. I want peace. I want somebody who will love me and not fame, who will care for me and think for me. This time it is love—real love, sincerity, and peace." Christmas came and went, as did the elections, and "real love" passed with the season.

Glen Kidston, English millionaire and the country's leading amateur sportsman, was soon courting Pola. Once more the actress led with a heart. Trying to better his own record in a

London-Capetown airplane flight, Commander Kidston was blinded by a duststorm, and he crashed into a mountainside.

It certainly looked more and more as though Pola's gypsy father knew what he was talking about when he said that the men she loved would meet with tragedy. Her former husband, Serge Mdivani, was dead, kicked in the head by a polo pony in 1935. No wonder the sight of white tuberoses, gypsy symbol of death, sent Polita into a near swoon.

Other days, however, brought other romances and alleged romances. They also brought the Nazi terror to a demoralized Europe. Pola retired to a villa in the south of France, where she occupied herself with gardening and Red Cross work. When matters continued to go from bad to far worse, Pola finally fled. In Lisbon she boarded the U.S.S. *Excalibur* with several hundred other refugees. Late in July, 1941, she arrived in New York harbor to a welcome far different from the tumult that had greeted her in 1922.

In Europe she had made another fortune, but again she had lost it. Virtually penniless, she began testing for film parts, riding to the studio in a taxi, living without a maid in a small apartment. "I have had some very bad luck," she summed up her state. "I have become very superstitious in the last two years because of the war. If I make a picture now after the great success I have made in the past, I want it to be something great."

Despair in Pola was always just a breath away from the sort of bravado she expressed here. The "something great" was a Universal film called *Hi Diddle Diddle,* with Adolphe Menjou. Pola's comedy role lampooned the temperamental Negri of the hectic days of the vamps and was well received.

Not until 1963 did Pola Negri make another film, a Walt Disney picture called *The Moonspinners,* with Hayley Mills, Eli Wallach, Joan Greenwood, and Peter McEnery. Originally intended as a spoof of the adventure-suspense genre, the picture never found its proper level. Pola Negri's delineation of an eccentric Egyptian multimillionairess with an unscrupulous passion for collecting jewelry was one of its redeeming features. As Madame Habib, she looked appropriately exotic, performing in one atmospheric scene on a yacht with her own pet cheetah. The accent, which detracted from her performance in a starring role, was here almost an asset.

After this comeback effort, Pola flew back to San Antonio, Texas, and the home she shared there with Margot West, a close friend of recent years. She also returned to the real estate business that she had built up, which was leading her to yet another fortune. When her companion died, leaving her a large lifetime income from a trust fund, Pola returned again to Hollywood and the film world she found so "irresistible." Still elegantly voluptuous, the many-lived Pola began one more chapter of an existence that can almost be described as monumental.

In her plush Beverly Hills mansion she lounged on the sofa, looking casually glamorous in bright red slacks, a black silk shirt, and a double strand of perfect pearls. She talked about her drama-drenched life and the forthcoming auto-biography—her third go-around in that genre—which would reveal all. To the inevitable questions about her multifarious love affairs she answered, "There were so many of them I scarcely remember." The one she did recall, as she had throughout the years, was Valentino. "He was the great love of my life, and his death, my greatest tragedy," she said. "We were drawn to each other from the very first. Both of us were unhappy. I had heard that he had expressed a great desire to meet me, but I avoided meeting him for some time because I had a feeling I would be disturbed and fascinated by this man. Finally a mutual friend brought us together, and after talking to him I had more of a premonition than ever that it would all end sadly. He was like a child, so trusting and lost in the wonderment of things."

But why think always of the past? The future beckoned. "I am a great character actress," Polita told the press, "and if I could get the right kind of role, I could go on forever—or at least as long as Lionel Barrymore did." If Hollywood did not act soon, she said, she would go to the continent and make another picture there. Then they would probably wake up and take notice of her talent.

Indeed, if the past is any guideline, Pola, having starred almost everywhere else in Europe, is likely to go to Soviet Russia. And if she goes, she is likely to be featured in a series of great epic films and given the Order of Lenin or some stupendous decoration. The premier of all the Russias will surely kiss her on both cheeks. There will be rumors of a tremendous love affair. Then Hollywood will notice.

4

MAE MURRAY

THE GIRL
WITH THE
BEE-STUNG LIPS

Today they were laughing, joyous. Arm in arm they walked, half waltzed their way through the park, the golden girl and the handsome dark Italian boy. Attendants recognized them and smiled. They came often. She was Mae Murray, a dancer who was beginning to be noticed, to make good on Broadway. His name was Rudolph Valentino. Only a few years ago he had come to America and taken a job as a landscape gardener in this same Central Park. Soon he had gone off to Maxim's, where lonely women paid to have him as a dancing partner. He was a gigolo.

But today they were gay. She was telling him exciting news. The day before, she had gone to practice new routines for her show at the Sans Souci, the cabaret in which she was heading the revue. Irving Berlin had come to see her. His first hit musical, *Watch Your Step*, was scheduled to go on as usual in the evening, but star Irene castle, wife of the famous Vernon Castle, was indisposed. Berlin didn't know whether she was ill or she and Vernon had had a fight. Whatever it was, she was temporarily out of the show. Could Mae take over with only four hours to prepare for the evening performance?

Without a moment's hesitation she said yes. She had come to

135

New York intoxicated by the dance craze that was sweeping the country. The Castles, who were her idols, had preceded her into the Sans Souci. She had seen them in *Watch Your Step* a dozen times and half-knew the routines already. All afternoon Berlin, a former singing waiter from Mike's in Chinatown, rehearsed her in the Castle Walk and the Turkey Trot. That night Mae performed the show's numbers as if they had been written for her. The audience showered her with applause. Berlin came backstage to offer congratulations. The producer, Charles Dillingham, kissed her on both cheeks. And she was going on again tonight.

She was on her way, she told Rudy, and when she really got there, she would help him make it too. Passersby watched the two graceful figures, Rudy lithe, sleek, his dark hair combed smoothly back, his wide-set eyes alternately playful and pensive; Mae, tiny and slim, always in motion, gesturing expressively, big, blue, innocent eyes set in a vivacious face, a pert nose, a cupid's bow mouth, riotous blond curls, chin held high. Even seated on a park bench Mae was in constant movement.

Sometimes Rudy would put his arm around her, press her lightly to him. She would tell him that romance was not for them, that they were friends. It was the year 1915. Rudy had only been in America two years, and he had just turned twenty. Mae was twenty-six, but she had already been married once and divorced. She had lived a good deal, experienced a lot.

Though her background was Belgian and Austrian—with a more distant sprinkling of Irish and Italian—her voice betrayed the slow cadence of the American South. Marie Adrienne Koenig was her real name, and she was born in Portsmouth, Virginia, on May 10, 1889. There was never much of a home for little Marie Adrienne. Her father died when she was very young, and her mother went to Europe, leaving her in the care of a strict grandmother, who felt that children should be seen and not heard. Marie was neither spanked nor scolded; she was ignored. One day she wandered into the street, intrigued by a hand-organ player with a monkey. As the ancient animal went through its routines, she imitated each movement, taking her first dancing lesson, eventually straying far from home. Her grandmother placed her in a convent to prevent a repetition of the incident.

All in vain. Marie ran away. She was found and sent to a boarding school near Chicago. There her roommate was training to go into the theater. The girl's dreams soon became her own. Marie left the school and took a job in a Chicago chorus line. Manhattan, however, was the center of the great dance and cabaret vogue of those pre-World War I days. To New York went Marie Koenig with a new name of her own choosing, Mae Murray.

She was not to keep it long. William Schwenker, Jr., son of a millionaire manufacturer, pursued and married her. In a furnished room she cooked their meals on a hotplate and tried to make up to him for the home he had lost (his family disapproved of their union). The marriage soon broke up. Mae never liked to speak of it afterward.

Her career became her obsession and dance its focus. Her convent and boarding school background proved inadequate as training grounds, so it was not easy to get a job. Mae decided to take a drastic step. Pooling every resource, she boarded a boat to Europe. In Paris she watched day after day, night after night, as dancers executed the latest steps. After two weeks she returned to New York with a thorough mastery of the pericot, the maxixe, and the tango. Her career began to take flight.

She won a small part in a musical comedy. The following year, 1908, saw her performing in the Ziegfeld *Follies*. The show's chorines were chosen to represent the ideals of famous illustrators of the time, Charles Dana Gibson, Harrison Fisher, Nell Brinkley, and others. Mae became the Nell Brinkley Girl. She repeated as Nell the following season and also landed a part in the production of *Her Little Highness*. When the manager of the Sans Souci caught her solo work in the show, he hired her for his cabaret, where she became the headliner. Irving Berlin saw her there, and now she was fulfilling her dream, dancing with Vernon Castle on Broadway.

She was indeed on her way but still unaware of how dizzying the pace of success would soon become. For three weeks she replaced Irene Castle in *Watch Your Step*, long enough to be seen by key people in the New York theater, including Florenz Ziegfeld. The great impresario offered his onetime chorine a featured number in his new review.

The Ziegfeld *Follies of 1915* carried a stellar cast, which included W.C. Fields, Ed Wynn, black comedian Bert Williams, Ina Claire, and George White. Beautiful dark-haired Olive Thomas, destined for early tragedy, was in the show, as were the lovely blonde Justine Johnstone and Ann Pennington of the splendid legs. Mae Murray, of the bee-stung lips and baby blue eyes, rounded out the cast.

Her number was typical of the show's opulence. As a Persian princess she was carried on stage wrapped in a brilliantly ornate rug. Dancing beside a limpid pool against a background of curved gold walls and a cobalt blue sky, she was seen by the prince, who wooed her. At first she encouraged him; then she changed her mind. To escape his continued entreaties she ran up a spiral of stairs and hurled herself over the wall.

Mae was also cast in *Merry Pickum*, a film sequence that travestied Hollywood. An obvious takeoff on Mary Pickford's charms, the bit showed that cameras could be as kind to Mae as the klieg lights had been. In the audience, motion picture pioneer Adolph Zukor was quick to see her potential. The next day he wrote asking to see her. A fur merchant turned nickolodeon operator, he had recently made a name for himself by importing and distributing a film of Sara Bernhardt as Queen Elizabeth. Mae had not heard of him, however. She was a star of the celebrated *Follies*, and films were considered a novelty that was likely to pass. She threw his letter into the wastebasket.

Certainly the reception accorded her on opening night justified her self-confidence. Enthusiastic applause greeted her Persian dance; the film sequence hit just the right note. Afterward in the dressing room there were flowers from the producer, from admirers such as Otto Kahn, the Wall Street tycoon, and from people with names she had never heard of.

Ziegfeld's wife, Billie Burke, offered congratulations, as did producer Charles Dillingham, Vernon Castle, and George M. Cohan. Broadway star Jeanne Eagels sent a note, and Rudolph Valentino came to the dressing room to say how wonderful she had been.

For Mae it was the beginning of exuberantly good times. No one in New York was more adored than the fabulous *Follies* girls; café society, titled foreigners, financiers, and politicians courted them. Invitations to exclusive balls, flowers, and expensive gifts were theirs for the asking. Millionaire playboy Tommy Manville waited at the stage door for pretty Florence Uber. Newspaper magnate William Randolph Hearst nightly bought two seats for the show—one for his hat and coat—to see Marion Davies. Olive Thomas was often at the side of Mary Pickford's handsome brother Jack. Ann Pennington and Marilyn Miller had their choice of well-heeled suitors. For the graceful and sensuous Mae Murray all doors opened. There were parties given by Whitneys, Vanderbilts, and Astors, by "Diamond Jim" Brady, by lumber kings and laxative kings, by gold mine owners.

One of the names she had at first not recognized was becoming familiar. Wealthy broker Jay O'Brien, called the Beau Brummel of Broadway, was waging a persistent courtship. She was attracted, confused, and sometimes repelled by his unorthodox behavior, his unannounced arrival at parties where she was dancing the night away, his violent bouts of jealousy.

So ardently did he pursue her that she began to feel threatened. She met the situation with a tactic she had used before: she ran away. Adolph Zukor was the means of her escape. Friends advised her at least to see this man who was offering stage performers large sums to come to Hollywood and make motion pictures. Mae's San Souci salary had been $30 a week. Ziegfeld only paid her $50 to start, later raising it to $175. The high-flying Zukor's offer was for a beginning $300, with a guarantee of $1,000 per week at the end of two years. Mae signed his contract and left for Hollywood in 1916.

In New York her star had risen fast and shone with a fresh

luster, but Hollywood looked at her with a jaundiced eye. She had neither dramatic stage nor motion picture experience. She was a dancer, a scant qualification for filmmaking. When she insisted on music to set the mood for her scenes, she was thought to have illusions of grandeur; either that, or perhaps she was a trifle daft, to use a term of the time.

Those fast-paced early months were not easy for a *Follies* star to go to the silent screen. For her film debut Famous Players-Lasky put her in *To Have and to Hold*, with Wally Reid, who had just played a key role in D.W. Griffith's great epic, *The Birth of a Nation*. This was swiftly followed by *Sweet Kitty Belairs*, a gentle comedy about the reigning favorite of an Irish regiment; *The Dream Girl*, a rags-to-riches story directed by young Cecil B. DeMille; and *The Big Sister*, in which Mae again played a waif surrounded by sordid characters.

The intensely competitive Hollywood scene was cold and unfriendly. The klieg lights were harsh, the directors often more so. Mae was a dancer, and her feet would sometimes not stand still, moving involuntarily into a light step that she felt expressed the character. Frowns and dismay greeted her improvisations. For one scene in which she was expected to register surprise a gun was shot off near her head. The whole atmosphere was a far cry from the adulation and gaiety she had known as a *Follies* favorite.

With her fifth film, *The Plow Girl*, things took a turn for the better. To direct this story, of an innocent farm girl in the African veldt, the studio selected Robert Leonard. An immediate sympathy sprang up between the big red-haired Irishman and his star. Each listened to the other's thoughts, and filming became a pleasant collaborative effort. The harmony began to extend to after hours, to dinners, to evenings spent together.

At this moment Jay O'Brien reappeared on the scene. Already jealous in New York when Mae performed her exotic dance in a theater, he was violently upset now that hundreds of thousands could see her on the screen. He had come to bring her activities to a halt by marrying her. As Mae later remembered it, their first evening together ended before a preacher, with Jay pointing a hidden gun at her head to insure the ceremony's completion. At the sp ·rited wedding supper her protests led to a shouting quarrel and to her escape through a ladies' room window. For a time the cloak and dagger atmosphere prevailed. The studio secreted her in her dressing room and provided an armed guard at the door. Not long after the subdued O'Brien returned east, and the marriage was dissolved.

Mae had serious misgivings about her early films, but they won wide approval. "Mae Murray would thrill you in five reels of the Constitution of the United States," a reviewer said of her performance in *The Plow Girl*. Bob Leonard was credited with much of the film's success. To him the studio entrusted her succeeding efforts: *On Record, A Mormon Maid*, which told of believers' efforts to convert outsiders, *The Primrose Ring*, about a children's nurse who is crippled and retreats to the fantasy world she has created for others, and *At First Sight*, a comedy in which Mae escaped from the clutches of a debonair cad scheming to marry her for her money.

Although she was already making $1,250 per week, Mae was dissatisfied. She wanted artistic direction to be in her own hands and Leonard's. The studio gave in, granting the two their own unit under the Bluebird label. Together they continued their happy collaboration with a skein of films that included: *The Princess Virtue, Face Value, The Bride's Awakening, Her Body in Bond, Modern Love, Danger—Go Slow, The Scarlet Shadow, What Am I Bid?, Big Little Person*, and *The Delicious Little Devil*.

In *The Delicious Little Devil* Mae made good on an old promise. Hearing that her old friend Valentino was having a bad time, she sent for him and cast him opposite her. He played the son of a millionaire contractor, in love with a nightclub entertainer whose provocative dancing alternately allured and embarrassed him. Dismayed because she was said to be a Parisian with a racy past, he was relieved to find she was only impersonating this notorious woman to further her career, that in reality she was a little girl from the slums—indeed, from the same neighborhood where he himself grew up and where their fathers once worked together as bricklayers.

The winning pattern of Mae Murray's screen image was crystallized in this film. Dance was henceforth an integral part of every picture. Spinning like a top, she was sensual but gay, flirtatious but at the same time basically decent and good. There was about her dainty, wistful figure a childlike quality of innocence. As her career continued, the innocence was to receive less emphasis, and the vivacious, the piquant, the lightly irresponsible aspects of the heroine moved to the fore.

Along the way Mae married Robert Leonard, a move that made scarcely a change in their screen-oriented way of life. Their professional paths diverged briefly. Leonard moved over to Cosmopolitan to direct another former *Follies* star, Marion Davies. Mae, her salary up to $1,750 per week, made *Twin Pawns* and *A.B.C. of Love* for Pathe under Leonce Perret's direction, and then *On with the Dance, The Right to Love*, and *Idols of Clay*, for George Fitzmaurice at Famous Players-Lasky. After this hiatus, the husband and wife team reunited for a series of films, which were among the most successful of Mae's ever-ascending career. Leonard gradually reduced the dialogue that flashed on the screen. Logical script sequence and pantomime took over. Spectacular dance prologues were used to set an effective mood for the action to follow.

In *The Gilded Lily* Mae made her entrance out of an enormous basket of balloons, her costume consisting of spangles, a jeweled G-string, and a small hat set at a rakish angle. Playing a Broadway club hostess, she began a dance designed to fascinate the young man who wanted to marry her but who was opposed in his wishes by his mother. The movements expressed the feelings of an unhappy woman, piqued at this interference, disillusioned because she saw that he loved the gilt and not the lily. A final frenzied whirl said that she was determined to hold him even by the weapons she despised.

Peacock Alley, Mae's first film for the surging Metro studio, cast her as Cleo, a light-hearted, talented, but vain entertainer who has all Paris at her feet. When she marries a young American businessman and returns with him to his home, her beauty and elegance stir up envy. Her husband is forced into crime to supply her wants, and not until he lands in jail does she wake up to reality. Meanwhile, she has had ample occasion to wear resplendent skin-tight outfits and to do sensuous dances with a lavish peacock costume that is topped off by a crest of aigrettes.

Fascination had Mae playing Dolores De Lisa, the high-spirited, irresponsible dancing daughter of a Spanish father and an American mother. In *Broadway Rose*, the heroine, a gifted dancer (what else?) married a lad of wealth only to find him a moral weakling. She then turned to the country boy who had loved her all along. *Jazzmania* was a Graustarkian tale that succumbed to the popular vogue for the costume play. *The French Doll* came next, followed by *Fashion Row*, with Mae in the dual role of Olga Farinova, dark-haired toast of Broadway, and Zita, the peasant sister who comes to join her in America. In *Mademoiselle Midnight* Mae played a Mexican siren; *Circe*, written especially for her by famed author Blasco Ibanez, continued the same basic mold.

If these fantasies and escapist dramas made Mae Murray one of the most popular and highest-paid stars in Hollywood, it should not be assumed that each effort was greeted with unreserved praise. Rare was the critic who could resist her beauty of face and body or the ravishing, often bizarre costumes and head-dresses that were her trademark. Her acting, often fluttery and mannered, was another matter, as were the type casting and the creaky, repetitive plots.

"Some like her affectations," wrote one critic, "but for others they are like hayfever and earthquakes and other things that must be endured." *Mademoiselle Midnight*, said the *New York World*, "reeks of old subterfuges, roaring coincidences, and melodrama. . . . Miss Murray . . . registers coyness by a minuet and eternal devotion by waltzes." "Mae Murray Plot Version Six," a magazine reviewer summed up a succeeding film. "It's the one in which she is a very virtuous dancer—she may skip about clad in georgette and a smile on the stage, but in her home life she is an Elsie Dinsmore, nothing less and nothing more." Playwright Robert Sherwood, reviewing for the *New York Herald*, called *Jazzmania* a "stupid picture, over-elaborate, incoherent." Nonetheless, he said, Mae's form was her fortune, and her beaded underthings were sufficient in themselves to insure vast popularity for the film. The otherwise critical *World* wrote of the same film, "There seems to be no one now acting before the camera who can put so much significance into a wink as Mae Murray can. Certainly the modern wiggle dance never rises to such importance as it does when she performs it." Overdone, many said of Mae's efforts, but when the dancing began, all was forgiven.

In any event, success in Hollywood was measured by the box office and reflected in a skyrocketing salary. Metro offered Mae $7,500 a week. She was at the height of her career, and she well knew it. She named her Metro production unit Tiffany because of the top-drawer elegance the name conveyed. Many Tiffany films were made at the specially-built studios on New York's West 44th Street: others, such as *Jazzmania*, were filmed in Hollywood. In both cities Mae cut a striking figure during these early years of the Roaring Twenties.

"Glamour is electric life, high voltage life," she proclaimed. "Success is initiative plus timeliness." Mae had it all. For her West Coast home she set up housekeeping on Adelaide Drive with a vast menagerie of cats, monkeys, a leopard cub, dogs (a St. Bernard *and* a Great Dane), and an aviary. One of her routine expenses at the spacious Spanish-style hacienda was a masseuse, whom she paid $250 a week to keep her famous dancing legs in shape. To the studio she commuted sometimes in a sleek canary yellow Pierce-Arrow, sometimes in a cream-colored Rolls Royce cabriolet with a black patent leather interior, with fittings of solid gold and cloisonne and two attendants in cream-and-black uniforms seated on the box. Extravagant parties were a regular event. For one such diversion, Mae ordered dummies made to resemble some of her co-players. Each dummy was cast in a mold of inebriation and placed in the garden. Entering guests were astonished to find a drunken Mary Pickford lying under a bush and a sozzled Charlie Chaplin propped up against a bench.

When filming in New York Mae and her husband lived in a sumptuous apartment at Des Artistes, overlooking the Central

Park she knew so well. Often she would walk to work through the park. At the end of the day attendants would see her familiar silhouette on horseback, riding at breakneck pace down the cindered paths to release the tensions of the working day. The apartment, with its own ballroom, swimming pool, and dumbwaiter service, played host to gala soirées, the solid gold china representative of the lavish trappings. There were parties, too, at friends' houses, or nights on the town, dancing at Romany Marie's and the Central Park Casino, listening to jazz at the Cotton Club, visits to speakeasies such as Jack and Charlie's 21, the onetime banker's plush home known as the Mansion, or the Club Napoleon, a favorite of musical comedy stars. Dancing, roller-skating, drinking bootleg gin, everyone was spinning like a top during this Era of Wonderful Nonsense.

"You could say we were like golden dragonflies suspended over a swamp," Mae said later. "We seemed to be suspended effortlessly in the air, but in reality our wings were beating very, very hard, very, very fast, so fast they were invisible. . . ."

Mae felt that the time had come to jazz up her gloomy convent background. *Photoplay*, leading chronicler of the foibles and fantasies of film stars, was the obvious medium. "I ran away always," she told its reporter. "Once I heard music in the streets of Paris, and I followed it, broke from the other children and followed the music all the way to the Sacre Coeur. I took off my shoes and danced to the bank until it was dark. Then I told the gendarmes I was lost and which was my convent, and they took me back."

Having shifted her youth to romantic Paris, she proceeded to embroider her birth. Her father was a sea captain who died when she was five, she said, and she was born on his boat. When *Photoplay*'s interviewer said he had quite a different biography in his files, Mae persevered: "I was born on my father's boat whilst at sea. I've never had any name save my own, Mae Murray." Compared to the tales fabricated by Theda Bara and her publicists, these inventions were tame.

For Mae, the golden girl of an incredibly gaudy period, the halcyon days would continue and grow even more dazzling—

before drawing to a grim close. At the moment her marriage to Robert Leonard was in trouble. Though their mutual attraction was great, her feeling for him was more companionate than passionate. In August, 1924, a quarrel led to a trial separation. The following year the marriage was dissolved with mutual declarations of affection and even love. "I am madly in love with Bob. I always shall be," Mae told the press. "Mae continues to occupy a place in my heart that no other woman could take. I shall never marry again," said Leonard. Mae was to marry again within a year. Before that event she was to score what was at once the most tormenting and the most prestigious success of her career.

Metro cast her in the film version of *The Merry Widow*, Franz Lehar's popular operetta. It told of Prince Danilo's love for Sally, the little dancing star of an American touring musical, of the opposition of his father, the king of a small European country, and of the villainous Crown Prince Miriko leering in the background, awaiting his chance to step into a closeup with Sally. To everyone's surprise, Erich Von Stroheim, justly famed for his productions of *Blind Husbands* and *Greed*, was called in to direct. While the frothy Lehar work seemed a most unlikely choice for his staid talent, Mae was aware that her artificial poster-girl dramas were wearing thin. Never had she bargained, however, for the uncompromising Von Stroheim.

In advance of filming she made a hurried trip to Vienna. She engaged the dancing master who had trained the original production's corps de ballet, learning from him each nuance of timing, each detail of dress. Fortified with her knowledge, she returned to Hollywood, stopping off in New York to scoop up a young Syrian named Adrian to design her clothes.

When she proposed the upcoming John Gilbert as her Prince Danilo, producer Irving Thalberg countered with veteran Norman Kerry. His choice was supported by Von Stroheim, but Mae won this first battle, since her contract gave her approval of the leading man.

For a time it was her only victory. Whereas she saw the Lehar story in terms of court intrigue, a love story, and the romantic waltz, Von Stroheim had in mind a vastly different concept. It was his plan to scoop beneath what he viewed as a superficial veneer, to apply his technique of penetrating realism to expose a core of European decadence. Aiming for social significance, he planned to throw out altogether the lilting "Merry Widow Waltz."

As filming progressed, Mae would sometimes ask for a closeup, but Von Stroheim would scornfully refuse. Deemphasizing the gaiety and romance, he dwelt upon the sordid aspects of continental court society. In one scene he had a lecherous old baron drool over Mae's feet until finally, in revulsion, she fainted. Von Stroheim insisted that the man was a foot fetishist and his perversion had to be shown. Chamber pots were made clearly visible in episodes set in the royal chambers. If a lady-in-waiting had a shadowy moustache, the camera was trained to catch it.

The director's realism saw to it that undergarments for soldiers in the film were marked with the coat of arms of a mythical country. He spent more than $10,000 for the designing of special military medals. In one scene he waited so long for a dog to sneeze that several exhausted extras passed out.

Battling each inch of the way, Mae injected into each reel some of the footage she wanted. She even prevailed in the matter of the famous waltz, which was reinstated in the plot line—not, however, without an incident in which Gilbert stumbled and Von Stroheim made sarcastic remarks about his two stars' acting abilities. At the end of her patience, Mae rushed at him, shouting that he was a dirty Hun. Gilbert wanted to quit, but she prevailed upon him to stay. She herself threatened a walkout unless Von Stroheim apologized. Halfheartedly he complied; then he himself withdrew. The film, a staggering ninety reels, was finished without a director and with everyone near nervous collapse.

Mae fled to Europe to recuperate. On her return she found that Wid Gunning, publisher of a Hollywood film weekly, had been called in to cut the enormous footage. His editing had captured enough of both the Von Stroheim realism and her romantic touches to win wild acclaim, to make it one of the great hits of 1925. "I am happy to say that Wid Gunning has left all objectionable trash shot in the picture on the cutting room floor," Mae said in a parting shot at Von Stroheim.

To her great satisfaction the "Merry Widow Waltz" was sweeping the nation. And despite contrary prognoses, John Gilbert made a dashing Prince Danilo as he guided his partner through the sweeping, gliding, swirling steps of the dance. Mae held her pretty head high, the train of a low-cut black velvet gown draped over her arm, the gown itself floating from diamond strands that met a glittering necklace about her neck.

"If one touched on all the fine points of *The Merry Widow*, one would write columns about it," said the *New York Herald Tribune*'s Harriette Underhill. Mae and John Gilbert came in for high praise, while Von Stroheim's direction was called peerless. In fact, concluded the ecstatic review, this was the first musical play to be successfully transferred to the screen.

"I do not think that Mae Murray has ever given a coherent, illusion-provoking performance before," wrote the *New York Sun*. "Here she donates a brilliant piece of romantic acting." The *New York Review* also sang Mae's praises: "The light, jiggling personality we have seen on the screen so many times does not appear in this characterization, and in its place Miss Murray gives us one of a sympathetic, appealing quality that she has never before let us have reason to believe she possessed. . . . She should let this new Mae Murray become a fixture."

Success was sweet. Back in Hollywood, Mae laughed and danced and entertained on a scale that reminded people of the days of Roman banquets. Several months later Pola Negri gave a birthday party, and Mae met the man who was to dominate much of the rest of her life.

The well-built David Mdivani, with his round face, wavy blond hair parted in the middle, and large cupid's bow lips, really looked a good deal like a larger version of Mae herself. The M in Mdivani was silent, but David was not. He was a prince

Mae Murray

Mae Murray as a Ziegfeld *Follies* girl, 1914.

For her film debut Famous Players-Lasky put Mae in *To Have and to Hold,* with Wallace Reid.

"The Girl with the Bee-Stung Lips" took a beating in *The Dream Girl* (1916), a rags-to-riches story directed by young Cecil B. DeMille.

Mae in *Broadway Rose* (right), a 1922 Tiffany-Metro production.

Mae and Earl Foxe in *The French Doll,* 1923.

Mae played the title role of *Circe, the Enchantress* in 1924 (top right).

The French Doll (top left).

Mae saunters through her gardens while making *Mademoiselle Midnight* (bottom left). Bottom right: Roy D'Arcy and John Gilbert with Mae in *The Merry Widow*.

Top and bottom: Mae Murray and
John Gilbert in *The Merry Widow*.
The story told of Prince Danilo's
love for Sally, the dancing star of
an American touring musical.

Top: Prince David Mdivani, Mae Murray,
Prince Serge Mdivani, Mrs. John McCor-
mack, and Mr. and Mrs. Rex Thomas attend
a Hollywood party after the completion
of *Peacock Alley*.

Left: Mae in her dressing room during her
vaudeville tour, just after completing the
sound version of *Peacock Alley*.

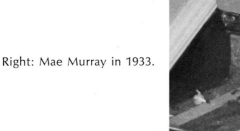

Right: Mae Murray in 1933.

Mae Murray in 1950 with producer
Ralph Straub.

Mae in 1964. Living just a block
from Grauman's Chinese Theatre,
she was often accompanied by a
young film enthusiast, who would
take her to lunch and a matinee.

of Georgia, he told Mae, a country with records dating back 200 years before Christ and now incorporated into Russia. The Mdivani title itself went back to 1752. He was one of five children of a general, Prince Zachary, and his Polish wife, famous for her beauty. Prince Zachary had been aide-de-camp to Czar Nicholas of Russia. During the darkest days of the Bolshevik Revolution the family had escaped from its vast estates in Georgia and fled to Paris, leaving behind their confiscated oil fields and other valuable properties. The three sons of the family had come to America. Serge and David had gone to work as laborers in the California oil fields. Their royal lineage gave them access to many of Hollywood's best houses, but the deplorable fact was that they were broke.

Mae listened to the unfolding of this tale with sympathy—but little else. For the prince it was the beginning of a courtship of unrelenting passion and fury. At the end of the party he hid in one of Mae's closets. She found him and asked him to leave. For several weeks she refused his calls. At the end of that period she discovered him on her front walk with slashed wrists. The wounds were superficial, but the melodramatic gesture registered. The courtship proceeded. Finally she agreed to an automobile ride in Mdivani's ancient jalopy. The prince went beyond the scheduled route, to a hunter's cabin in the Hollywood hills. Virtually kidnapped, Mae refused to speak. David, on the other hand, spoke, cried, cajoled, was alternately ardent and abject, the little child in need, the dashing European prince. At the end of four days, she wilted under this intense psychological onslaught and married him in the Church of the Good Shepherd in Beverly Hills. Pola Negri was the matron of honor, Rudolph Valentino, the best man.

It was the first of a series of nuptials to replenish the Mdivani family exchequer and give the three sons the onerous title, "the marrying Mdivanis." Elder brother Serge followed David's lead by steering Pola Negri to the altar the following year. Later he entered into other marriages, with opera singer Mary McCormic and Louise Van Alen, an Astor heiress. Younger brother Alexis preceded Serge as the husband of the same Louise Van Alen, and when that marriage was dissolved, he went on to marry Woolworth heiress Barbara Hutton.

During their first years together Mae and her prince were considered one of the happiest couples in Hollywood. They called in Frank Lloyd Wright to design a palatial home at Playa del Rey, where they set up housekeeping. Mae pursued her career, and her efforts continued to meet with success.

In *The Masked Bride* she appeared with Roy D'Arcy, Basil Rathbone, and Francis X. Bushman, saving the tired story line with her dancing. Critics bemoaned the fact, however, that she had gone back to pursing her lips, making what they called goo-goo eyes, and holding her madonna-like expression for long and frequent close-ups. Mae herself was said to be dissatisfied with *Valencia*, another mythical kingdom story, and with *Altars of Desire*.

During her trip to the continent to research *The Merry Widow* she had been pursued by Universum Film Akti-engesellschaft, the big German production company better known as UFA. Offered a lucrative contract, she signed and was given $75,000 as a bonus. William Randolph Hearst immediately told her that his giant newspaper chain would boycott her films. Movie czar Will Hays implored her to break the contract tendered by this top studio of a competitive country. Knowing that films without proper American distribution were doomed financially, Mae returned her bonus, and the agreement with UFA was canceled.

Next it was her husband who asked her to walk out on a contract. After basking for a time in his wife's success, David Mdivani began to resent her career, to find it bruising to his powerful ego. Sex appeal was a major ingredient in all her film roles. Like Jay O'Brien before him, he increasingly felt the impropriety of these appearances. He wanted his wife to himself.

Succumbing to his persuasive powers, Mae packed their trunks. Together they embarked for Europe, neglecting to notify Metro Goldwyn Mayer. Studio head Louis B. Mayer cabled his star, ordering her to return at once for a picture. His command was ignored. He was never to forget it.

Over the years Mae had spent money, but she had also managed to save a good deal. For the projected stay on the continent she ordered close to half a million dollars transferred to accounts in Paris. She and Mdivani proceeded to splurge it in two high-flying years.

In Europe, David, the master of his itinerant house, felt more at home, but his jealousy continued. When a New York agent offered Mae $25,000 a week for an American dance tour, she accepted. It would be a way to recoup her finances and also to temper David's domination, which was becoming oppressive. He reacted with extreme anger, remaining in Europe alone, making the ocean trip to join her only when his mood had changed.

An extraordinary circumstance of the foreign sojourn came to light when Mae returned to New York—she was a mother with a year-old baby! To reporters who besieged her she was cool, refusing to give the place or date of birth, although the mystery baby was living in her home, guarded by a Japanese nurse. Eventually she satisfied the public's demand for details. The child, a boy named Koran, had been born in Europe. She had kept his existence a secret for more than a year, fearing that the revelation might harm her career.

Rather than bring harmony to the failing marriage, Koran, whose name was chosen because it connoted knowledge, eventually became another item in a growing list under dispute. The dance tour offended Mdivani even more than Mae's films. Violent arguments ensued, draining the energy she needed for her strenuous act. Quarrels were followed by tearful and tender reunions. When Mdivani said that he needed money to explore for oil on their properties, Mae acceded to his request. With a background in the field, the prince actually made a number of strikes. Success bolstered his ego, and for a time the household was on a smoother footing.

Only for a time. Dancing and her career were integral parts of

Mae's life. Against her husband's objections she pursued them. With Jason Robards, Sr., she made a talkie remake of *Peacock Alley*, which Louis B. Mayer tried unsuccessfully to block. As a speaking performer Mae was less effective than in pantomime. Still, the film was a modest success. She and Lowell Sherman put up their own money to co-star in *Bachelor Apartment*, with Mae in the role of a vivacious Park Avenue temptress, and in *High Stakes*, which had her playing a guileless golddigger. Mayer, a great power in films, was not to be denied. He exerted all his influence to prevent further United States productions by the star who had crossed him. His blackballing efforts forced Mae and Sherman to England. Their plans there were beginning to jell when Sherman suddenly died.

For the golden dragonfly of the twenties, the swamp below was beginning to appear menacingly close. After a decade of triumphs and public adulation, the cameras turned away from the doll-like face with the bee-stung lips, from the dainty feet that could dance up a baby cyclone. A Depression was at hand. There was no work, either for Mae or for thousands of others, feature players cast aside by the talkies and extras who roamed the streets of Hollywood as the film industry retooled.

The marriage to Mdivani was no longer even intermittently happy. Despondent and bewildered, Mae asked her prince for a divorce. When he refused, saying that the marriage was Catholic and could not be dissolved, she offered money, the commodity which had often solved their problems in the past. The prince laughed. She had no money, he told her. He reminded his startled wife that she had granted him power of attorney over her estate. Monies had been transferred to his name. She had nothing. He, in fact, would give her money if she returned, in the proper manner, to the family hearth.

The time for compromise had long since passed. Mae began divorce proceedings, charging extreme cruelty. The action asked for no alimony but petitioned for custody of their son. "I am gaining something that is more important than money—my freedom," said Mae.

At a fashionable Hollywood hotel she hovered over teacups with opera singer Mary McCormic, who had brought a separate maintenance suit against David's brother, Serge Mdivani. The two women joined in submitting affidavits to the court. Mae charged her husband with collecting more than $500 a month from his interests in three oil companies but failing to support her. Moreover, she alleged that she had put up money amounting to a one-third share in these concerns, enabling him to buy them. To these charges she added unreasonable jealousy.

Mary McCormic's affidavit said that she also advanced money for her husband's business ventures, which had prospered. She charged that Serge had struck her, blackened her eye, and locked her in her room. She further stated that of a $40,000 loan Serge had only paid back $500. She asked a decree granting $600 a month support plus an accounting of community property.

The two plaintiffs were discussing their marital woes when the princes returned from Europe, where they had gone for the wedding of their third brother, Alexis, to Barbara Hutton. "If we're not wanted, we won't stick around," Serge told the press at the dock in New York. Mary's charge that Serge had blackened her eye only proved he was a he-man, he added. As for his borrowing money and not paying it back, that was laughable. "How can a man borrow money from his wife?" he asked. "If one has money, the other uses it." The two brothers said that they would not contest the divorces, save for the matter of alimony in Serge's case.

On October 24, 1933, Mae was divorced in Los Angeles Superior Court, waiving all claims of alimony but gaining custody of her son. She signed a property settlement, which provided a $5,000 annual trust fund income for Koran.

In November the palatial home at Playa Del Rey was auctioned off to satisfy a $60,000 judgment. Four other pieces of real estate later went under the hammer. In January, 1934, Mae Murray, once among the highest paid of Hollywood stars, instituted bankruptcy proceedings. She charged the Princes Mdivani with embezzling money from their corporation, now in receivership. Earlier at a special meeting the stockholders, including Mae and Mary McCormic, had ousted them as officers and directors.

The bitterness between Mae and her former husband continued over the years and later burst back into the headlines. Meanwhile, she drew attention with other matters. In a suit against Tiffany Productions she asked for $300,000 allegedly due as her share of films made years ago. The suit was dismissed but not before a court scene in which Bertram Mayers, attorney for Tiffany, whispered to her, "Now you've got justice," and received a healthy slap in the face as his reward.

In June, 1934, Mae returned to Broadway, but with a difference. She followed Gladys George in *The Milky Way*, a comedy about a milkman who is forced into the prizefight game and who winds up, by a fluke, becoming champion. Hugh O'Connell played the milkman, Brian Donlevy the real prizefighter, and Sam Levene, his manager. As the manager's mistress Mae wore stunning costumes, which she herself designed. Her opening night was rich with emotion. At the first sound of applause she rushed toward the footlights, spreading her arms in a gesture of love for the audience. "An all but indefinable something we rather thought went out with the silent screen has been recaptured," wrote one delighted critic.

Mae had brought glamour to Broadway, but in her remaining years there were to be only rare occasions to display it. Although it was a welcome novelty, the stage appearance generated little interest in her dramatic ability. Louis B. Mayer continued to blackball her. When she appealed to him at least to hear her side of the story, her letter went unanswered.

Finally in the mid-thirties came an offer to make three pictures in England for the sum of $100,000. Mae was ready to leave when a new wave of ill-fortune struck. Young Koran contracted an ear infection and was rushed to a hospital. A long series of operations were performed. As the illness wore on, Mae remained at his side, canceling the English contract. Piece by piece she was forced to sell her remaining possessions, jewels, furs, everything of value, to pay hospital bills. She was relieved when Koran became fond of Daniel Cunning, who had operated on him. Dr. Cunning, aware of her money problems, invited the boy to his family home near Albany, New York, where his sister Bessie could look after him.

With Koran cared for, Mae went again to look for work. She wrote each Hollywood studio but received no offer. In New York she made the rounds, also without success. Wandering between the two cities, she searched for an echo of that vanished era that she had helped to make glamorous. Every venture failed.

One nightmarish day she awoke to find the cupboard bare; she had not enough in her purse even to pay for her cheap hotel room. She packed a small hat bag with a jar of cold cream, a clean pair of stockings, and a change of lingerie. When evening came, she walked out to Central Park, where she had ridden horseback at full tilt when her star was high, where she had walked arm in arm with Rudolph Valentino. Rudy had had his own tragedy, had met his untimely death long years ago. Mae walked alone now, sat alone on a park bench as night fell, sat and dozed, dreamed strange troubled dreams—and finally looked up to see the dawn breaking. For three days she made the park her home, using its public restrooms to perform her toilet, sleeping on park benches. At the end of that time, weary and numbed, she went to friends for help.

Belatedly, in 1939, she sued David Mdivani for $12,000 a year child support, contending that he had never set up the trust fund from which Koran was to receive an income. Her deposition maintained that David had received various inheritances and had rebuilt his oil empire so that he was once again affluent and able to support his son.

When the case came up, the California court said that it would not make a decision without the boy's presence. Mae went to Albany to bring back Koran only to find the Cunnings completely opposed to turning him over. This led her to institute habeas corpus proceedings, which they countered.

The resulting court drama drew national headlines. The Cunnings said that Mae had shown little interest in her boy in recent years, that they could provide a better home for him than she. Sobbing, Mae told of how she had walked out of her marriage completely bankrupt, of the English contract she had been forced to give up due to Koran's illness, of the money that caring for him had taken. "From then on it became a fight for my health," she recounted, "a fight so that no one would know I hadn't any money, and a fight for 'face,' for it seems not to be attractive to be without money."

Once she had sold a $5,000 chinchilla coat for $150 to pay for one of Koran's operations, she testified. She had pleaded with David, but in vain, to assist her and to see his boy. Over the years she had corresponded with Koran on the best of terms, visiting him on holidays. However, when she had gone to the Cunnings just before instituting suit, they had refused to let her see him alone. Koran had appeared at the screen door and told her, "Mommy, they won't let me out."

After hearing testimony New York Supreme Court Justice Bergan ruled there was nothing against the mother morally or in any way to render her unfit as the child's custodian. But, he found, she seemed to have no means and no permanent home. As a result, he was leaving Koran with the Cunnings, with the proviso that Mae could renew her plea for his custody when her circumstances altered.

Reeling from this blow, Mae suddenly received support from California Superior Judge George Dockweiler. He decreed that Mdivani must pay her $400 a month to support Koran and that she was entitled to custody. The ruling stated, "It is most singular to note that he [Mdivani] would spend substantial sums for distant relatives and friends abroad, but with respect to his own flesh and blood he made no contribution for many years, other than a few paltry dollars he gave to his wife for their son's needs. This is indeed something the court can hardly understand, and for which the defendant gave no adequate explanations." With this proof that she could support her son, Mae again went East, hoping to convince Judge Bergan. To counter her, David Mdivani also came for the proceedings. On arrival, he said that he was pleased with Koran's home and the Cunnings' manner of rearing him. "What could be better for him than to be a regular American boy?" he asked, "I wouldn't want my son to know what it is like to be called 'a marrying Mdivani.' "

Koran's appearance on the witness stand spelled final defeat for Mae. "I want to remain with Bessie," he testified. "Tell the court why you want to stay with Bessie," the Cunnings' attorney said. "Because I am happy there," Koran replied. "I have a place to play and boys to play with."

The disaffection of her son was profoundly demoralizing for Mae. It was her feeling that the Cunnings disapproved on puritanical grounds of Hollywood and the way of life she represented. Koran, the son of a prince and a great motion picture star, never renewed close relations with either, preferring the name of his foster family and, later, the modest life of a small town businessman.

Although her life was running down, the pace of its decline steady, one more flamboyant triumph awaited Mae Murray. In 1941 showman Billy Rose opened a new review at his famed night club, the Diamond Horseshoe. *The Cavalcade of the Silent Screen* was directed by John Murray Anderson. Its headliners included gray-haired Carlyle Blackwell, one of the screen's earliest idols, and bosomy Nita Naldi, a leading vamp of the twenties, who read Kipling's "The Vampire." Gilda Gray demonstrated the shimmy, the dance that she had brought into national vogue, Lila Lee made a dramatic appearance, and Joe E. Howard, composer of "I Wonder Who's Kissing Her Now," sang the old-time favorite. These and others were warmly applauded as they came on stage.

But the aging star who brought patrons to their feet was the amazingly graceful Mae Murray dancing the "Merry Widow Waltz." Nostalgically gowned in the original black velvet with the trim draped over her arm, her chin held high as she swirled and glided and returned to her partner, she seemed to recapture another era, a lost time of measure and elegance. "They do love me, don't they?" she said as the applause swelled after her number. "It's always the same. I try to get into people's hearts, and I think I do."

When she repeated much of her act at the Hollywood Mocambo, she spoke of her greatest love. "There's something when I dance that strikes people. I haven't tried to define it," she said. "I feel close to God when I'm dancing."

Her nimble, restless feet saw less and less activity, however. From time to time there was still some nightclub work and a little radio and television, but there were also long periods of idleness. Back and forth between New York and California the former screen goddess wandered like a homeless bird, her hair as blonde as dyes could make it, a big floppy picture hat on her head, her bearing always regal, reminiscent of past grandeur, no matter how straitened her circumstances. When in New York she occupied a maid's room at Des Artists, her old apartment residence.

In 1960 she suffered a stroke, and thereafter her health continued to fail. In February, 1964, she was found in a confused state wandering the streets of St. Louis. Traveling by bus, she had apparently mistaken that city for her destination, New York. She was penniless. The Salvation Army came to her aid and put her on a Hollywood-bound plane. In August, 1964, she was admitted to the Motion Picture Country Home, and there, in March, 1965, she died quietly.

Did she have any regrets, she was asked not long before her death. "No, none at all," she answered. As for the adulation and glory she had once known, they were still a part of her and always would be. "Once you become a star," she said, "you are always a star."

In her last years she would sometimes visit the large collection of old film stills at New York's Museum of Modern Art. One young attendant was amused because of a curious scene that regularly took place. Looking at photos of herself, she would be serene until she came across a shot that displeased her. A frown would appear, and she would glance furtively about. Convinced that no one was watching, she would crunch the unflattering picture into a ball and shove it into her purse. For Mae Murray, the veteran of battles with Adolph Zukor, Louis B. Mayer, and Erich Von Stroheim, it was never too late to do a little cutting to improve a film.

5
CLARA BOW

THE "IT" GIRL

It was the middle of the night, and in her small, almost airless bedroom sixteen-year-old Clara Bow was sleeping fitfully, tossing, turning, half dreaming, half awake. A storm was passing over the Bay Ridge section of Brooklyn, with flashes of lightning and low rolls of thunder. In the next room were Clara's parents, and once she thought she heard footsteps in the hall. When they seemed to die away, she got up and pushed the window wide open, but the hot, humid night was still and oppressive. Clara went back to bed, stopping to peer through the dim light at the photographs on the wall, all of movie stars. There was handsome Wally Reid, with whom she was carrying on a long-distance, one-sided, hopeless love affair; and there was golden-curled Mary Pickford, Clara's greatest idol. The fan magazine photos showed Mary in her most popular films, each of which Clara had gone to see many times—*Rebecca of Sunnybrook Farm, Tess of the Storm Country, Pollyanna, Little Annie Rooney*. How beautiful Mary was! How romantic her life seemed to be!

There were photos, too, of Lillian Gish, Norma Talmadge, and many others. Smiling at the memory of the wonderful

161

adventures she had lived through with her screen favorites, Clara fell asleep.

Suddenly she was awake again and terrified. She felt something cold at her neck, saw her mother by the bed, a huge butcher knife in her hand. She was ranting at her, only half coherent, a wild look on her face, the knife pressing against Clara's neck. What was it she was saying? Something about Clara and motion pictures. She wouldn't have her daughter go into that terrible business. It was wrong and dirty. Nice girls wouldn't show themselves for other people, sometimes half undressed, work with crazy people who would take advantage. It was better not to have a daughter than to have her go into that world. It was better to be dead than get mixed up like that.

The pain of the knifepoint hurt Clara, but she didn't cry. She started to talk, her voice no more than a whisper at first. She wouldn't do anything her mother thought was wrong, she said. She loved her mother. She would be a good girl. Over and over she repeated the same reassurances. She would obey. She would be good, really and truly she would.

To her intense relief, she felt the knife's pressure diminish. She looked up to see tears running down her mother's face. Then the knife dropped to the floor. With cat-like speed, Clara darted from bed and ran to the door. Looking back she saw that her mother had not moved, was not pursuing, was sitting in weird silence. Nonetheless Clara went down the hall and locked herself in a small storage room. There she spent the stormy night stretched out on a makeshift cot.

As the long hours passed, thoughts raced through her head. What a strange world it was, one that never seemed to want her in the first place. She had learned that when she overheard a conversation between her parents. Her mother had lost two babies in childbirth and almost died herself. She was terribly upset and afraid when she found that another child, Clara, was on the way. The birth pains went on and on, with the mother's life and Clara's in the balance. Doctors fought gamely and finally saved them both.

Sometimes Clara wondered why. In their small upstairs flat,

her mother was always ill; she suffered from a nervous disease. There were fainting spells and depressions, trance-like states. Even when she was very young, Clara helped with the cooking, washing, and the other housework. She would never forget the evening that she heard screams and rushed downstairs. Johnny, a boy who lived next door, had gone too close to the fire. His hair was burning, and as he cried for help, Clara rolled a rug around him to put out the flames. It was too late. He died in her arms. It was like that, living in a tenement on a side street of Brooklyn. A babysitter would have kept Johnny from harm, but there was no money for babysitters.

There was never enough money. Clara's father was a waiter at Coney Island, also a carpenter and general handyman, but he kept losing his job. Clara could never understand how anyone could fire him. He was such a wonderful man, a strong, dark-eyed Scottish-Englishman. Clara felt deeply for her mother, longing to have her well, but it was her father she loved without reserve.

He was the one who helped her with the contest. Everybody else thought she was crazy, Clara Bow, the tomboy, carrot top, entering a beauty contest. To the neighbors she was more boy than girl. It was the way she dressed and acted, wearing boy's clothes, running around with boys. She could outrace all of them and hold her own in a fight if one occurred, which was practically every day. Sometimes she'd hitch a ride on the back of a fire engine. That was real speed, faster than the roller skates on which she liked to careen down the street. Short, pudgy, madcap Clara Bow in a beauty contest—who would believe it?

It happened when she read in *Motion Picture Classic* how simple it was: just send two photos with your name, age, and address. A committee of three magazine illustrators—Howard Chandler Christy, Harrison Fisher, and Neysa McMein—would first choose twenty girls from all those submitted. Each would be given a screen test, and one would win the Fame and Fortune Sweepstakes and be declared "The Most Beautiful Girl in the World." The only problem was the photos. The pennies Clara earned running errands were all spent on the movies. It was her father who came to her aid, handing over two dollars, taking her to a cheap photographer in the area. The man told her to untie the band that held the hair back out of her eyes. The waves of curly red looked different when they fell free. The man asked her how about a little smile. She smiled. Several weeks later she received a letter that said that she was one of the twenty to survive the first round. She would be given a screen test.

With her father, Clara went to 175 Duffield Street, Brooklyn, the editorial office of Brewster Publications. When she saw the other girls who were competing, she began to cry. They were beautiful, smartly dressed, artfully manicured. She was wearing an old sweater, a pair of scuffed shoes, and a skirt discarded by her mother. Her father held her hand and kept her from bolting when her name was called.

As she posed for the camera, a certain ingenuous quality, a youthful spontaneity came through. Her face was mobile, the luminous brown eyes alive, framed by long, provocative black lashes. Whereas the other girls tried to impersonate adult stars, she was young, fresh, vibrant. Under the heading "A Dream Come True," *Motion Picture Classic* published her photo and proclaimed her the winner of the 1921 Fame and Fortune Contest. "Her features are delicate and sensitive, particularly her mouth, which is red and curved, drooping prettily at the corners," read the caption. "She is slim and well-formed—just beginning to curve into womanhood. She is plastic, alert, young and lovely. Her name is Clara Bow."

While it promised much, the highly ballyhooed contest was slow in delivering. Its terms stated that the magazine would help the winner gain a role in films. The manner was hardly dramatic. "The most beautiful girl in the world" was sent to various casting offices with a letter of introduction. With the film industry in a postwar lethargy, Clara's arrival stirred little interest.

She was eventually given a small part in Christy Cabanne's *Beyond the Rainbow*, on the condition that *Motion Picture Classic* would plug the picture. When it played in the New York area, Clara invited her friends to the first showing. Her "plastic, alert" face was never seen. The tiny role had wound up on the cutting-room floor.

Despondent, Clara quit high school to work in a doctor's office. Hollywood receded from her mind. She was giving thought to secretarial school and to a new boyfriend when she received a surprise call. Director Elmer Clifton had seen her magazine photo. He wanted her for his new film, *Down to the Sea in Ships.*

A whaling epic made on location in New England, the film was an important breakthrough for Clara. While it starred Marguerite Courtot and Raymond McKee, her scenes came to the attention of B.P. Schulberg, a rising power in the film world. He sent a wire from Hollywood offering to put her under personal contract at $50 a week.

The opportunity was what she had dreamed of, but Clara hesitated. She felt guilty about her mother, who was increasingly ill. After finishing a bit part in *Enemies of Women* she decided to give up her career. She went home to tell her mother, but Sarah Bow no longer recognized her. In the morning she was dead.

For long weeks, Clara felt remorse and grief, and the Schulberg offer remained in abeyance. Finally Robert Bow persuaded her that her mother had not meant everything she had said in the last stages of her illness. She would want her daughter to have a career and success. She should go on. Clara finally signed the contract.

Into a papier mâché bag she put a suit of underwear trimmed with cheap lace, one pair of stockings, and a roughneck sweater. Her father took her to Grand Central Station, where she was met by her newly acquired agent, Maxine Alton. They boarded the train, Clara fearful, chewing gum, consoling herself with her portable phonograph and one scratchy record, "The Parade of the Wooden Soldiers." She played it over and over for most of the next five days, stopping only to visit other passengers, whom she beguiled with endless questions and staccato accounts of life in Brooklyn. Clara was still bright-eyed, but her agent was haggard and worn when they stepped off the train at Pasadena to do battle with the burgeoning film industry.

For some time Hollywood ignored the little redhead from Brooklyn, who continued to write long letters to the Answer Man in *Photoplay Magazine*.

Gradually a few small parts came her way, bits in Preferred Pictures productions of *Maytime, The Boomerang, Poisoned Paradise, Free to Love*, and *The Great Sensation*. Then came bigger roles in *Grit* and *Black Oxen*.

Her career was picking up steam. Each year the Western Associated Motion Picture Advertising Men selected a group of promising young actresses, who were then called Wampas Babies. Mary Astor, who also won a Fame and Fortune Magazine contest, was the winner in 1923. Colleen Moore, Bessie Love, Lillian Rich, Claire Windsor, and Lois Wilson had all been Wampas choices. The Wampas Babies of 1924 were soon forgotten, except for Clara Bow, who was selected as the girl who typified the flapper.

The following year Clara's mentor, B.P. Schulberg, went to Paramount Pictures as vice-president. He took Clara along, guiding her even higher. Ernst Lubitsch directed her in a 1925 production of *Kiss Me Again*, which was based on a popular Victor Herbert operetta. Marie Prevost and Monte Blue were in the cast. Although thin in story line, the film was directed with a sure light touch, and it scored a great success. *Dangerous Curves*, with Richard Arlen, added to Clara's reputation.

It was in 1926, however, that she catapulted to stardom. A celebrated English author precipitated her on the way. Elinor Glyn had written the runaway bestseller *Three Weeks* and other novels daring for their time. Her views on the relations between the sexes were featured in the large circulation magazines, and Hollywood imported her to write screenplays.

While she was visiting Clara on the set, she was struck by her vivacity and charm. "That girl has It," she said. When Clara asked what It meant, she replied cryptically, "You either have It or you don't." The press demanded a fuller explanation, and Glyn obliged. "There are few people in the world who possess

It," she said. "The only ones in Hollywood who do are Rex the wild stallion, actor Tony Moreno, the Ambassador Hotel doorman, and Clara Bow."

The endorsement from the popular sex oracle gave Clara a special place in the national spotlight. No one seemed to know quite what It was, but she definitely had it. She herself said It was the ability to give your undivided attention to the person you are speaking to. The dictionary soon defined It in terms of personal magnetism and charm.

During the year 1926 Clara displayed It in a brisk piece of buffoonery called *Kid Boots*, with Eddie Cantor, in *Children of Divorce*, with new leading man Gary Cooper, and in *Dancing Mothers*, adapted from a Broadway play and directed by Herbert Brenon. *Dancing Mothers'* plot dealt lightly with the twenties mania for dancing and drinking cocktails. As Kittens Westcort, Clara played a young flapper in love with an attractive scoundrel, a role taken by Conway Tearle. She goes blithely to his apartment, indifferent to what the butler thinks, snatches the cocktail shaker from his hand, and proceeds to throw the contents down her finely arched throat. A mere two thimblefuls fill her with almost uncontrollable gaiety, which is somewhat curtailed by the scoundrel's arrival. He is visibly annoyed; it turns out that he was awaiting the arrival of an older but more beautiful woman—Kitten's mother. The subsequent unfolding of the plot saw Clara go from incident to incident, always on the lookout for fresh mischief, for new ways to shock.

Ernest Torrence, Percy Marmont, and Eugene Pallette were some of the men she proceeded to vamp in *Mantrap*. The Victor Fleming production was based on a Sinclair Lewis novel. "Clara Bow is the flapperish wife, and the artful vagaries of that child of the big city when turned loose in the woods with nobody to practice on but a few trappers, are remarkable," said the *New York Times*. "As a wife who can't make her eyes behave, she runs away with everything," said *Photoplay*. "She is personality and sex appeal plus."

College boys became the object of prey in *The Plastic Age*, directed by Wesley Ruggles. The hero, Donald Keith, starts out as a studious youngster, adept at both scholarship and athletics, but gay fraternity dances and parties begin to take their toll. When attractive Cynthia Day, played by Clara, is added to the list of distractions, there is no longer any doubt that he will start losing on the sports field. Despite her liking for gaiety and bright lights, Cynthia decides to sacrifice herself and withdraw from his life. He triumphs in the big game, graduates, and wins her back with an embrace that knocks over their love seat.

"Eyes that would draw any youngster away from his books, and she knows how to use eyes, shoulders, and all the rest of her tiny self in the most effective manner," said the *Times*. "She radiates an elfin sensuousness."

To capitalize on the recently christened It Girl, Paramount put together a predictable package. Elinor Glyn was called in to write a screen comedy called *It*. Clarence Badger directed, and Antonio Moreno, who also had It, was given the male lead. While Paramount moguls failed to corner Rex the wild stallion or the Ambassador doorman, they induced the author herself to make an appearance in the film. She is dining at the Ritz when an acquaintance stops to ask about It. "It is a combination of nonself-consciousness and an indifference as to whether one is pleasing those around one," says Glyn. "If you have It, you can win any man you want." A moment later she caustically refers to two minor characters as "just a couple of Itless Its."

The familiar story dealt with a shopgirl and her employer. As poor girl Betty Lou, Clara works in a mammoth department store, where she first lays eyes on Cyrus Waltham, Jr., son of the owner. Although for her it is instant romance, he hardly notices her. Not so his friend Monty, who has in fact read Elinor Glyn's account of It in *Cosmopolitan* and sees that Betty Lou fills the bill. He invites her to dinner. While her interest in Monty is nil, Betty Lou determines to use him to reach Cyrus, Jr.'s, heart. For dinner she suggests the Ritz, much to Monty's surprise. "Shall we dress?" he asks, wondering what the little shopgirl will wear. "Don't be absurd. Of course," she replies, rushing upstairs to cut the neck and sleeves out of a black satin work frock, twisting some tulle around her head, and reappearing in a trice ready for the Ritz. Entering the elegant dining room, they're met by a haughty headwaiter who offers a corner niche. "I do not crave this table. When I'm in the swim, I want to be with the goldfish," says Betty Lou, and she is shown to the best corner.

Soon the hero enters, taking a nearby table, thus allowing Betty Lou to exercise her charms for him and the other customers. Her hair in bangs and coming far down her cheeks like two facing scythes, a thin line of mascara for eyebrows, with heavy lashes that invite attention, she remains perpetually in motion, bouncing, giggling, pulling a wishbone with Monty, uttering little gasps about each morsel of food. Finally the hero gets the message. He sees that Betty Lou has It, and he begins courting her. Success will be his but not before Betty Lou strums out a tune on a ukelele and drives home a lesson in how to treat someone who has It. Having taken her for a ride in his Rolls Royce roadster, Cyrus steals a quick kiss and receives a hard slap for his pains. "You're one of those Minute Men," cries the indignant shopgirl. "Try to kiss a girl the minute you're out with her."

The scenes were typical Clara Bow characterizations. Her behavior was daring and sometimes outrageous. Flirting and easy infatuation were the order of the day. Dancing, drinking, rouge, and lipstick were all accepted. Old-fashioned sexual inhibitions were thrown overboard, but to everything there was a limit. At a certain point the revelry stopped—when the hero went too fast, when the partying could endanger his career. Clara Bow was naughty, but underneath she was very nice.

Somewhat later, in Clara's private life, this limitation was to cause the Brooklyn Bonfire much anguish. For the moment she typified the emancipated flapper. No one quite knew where that word came from. At an earlier period, college coeds were called chickens, and perhaps flapper, a species of young wild duck, was a logical successor. Whatever the origin, Clara Bow represented better than anyone else the ideal girl of the twenties, the time of hot-cha, adolescent rebellion, and harum-scarum hilarity, of Prohibition and hip flasks, of short skirts and raccoon coats.

Under the caption "Spirit," Paramount sent out publicity photos that showed her with the wind in her hair, a half-smile on her lips. "Clara Bow is a living symbol of our idols—speed and pep. She moves all the time," wrote an analyst of the time. "Then, too, she has a thing we all prize highly, youth. Real youth. She must have been born with a fund of nervous energy that would run the dynamo of an electric plant."

Said another critic: "Clara Bow has, you know, more than a touch of mad, Byronic young genius."

Directors were ready to testify to Clara's professional ability. They bemoaned the fact that the public limited her range. It was the death scene in *Children of Divorce* that director Victor Fleming especially liked; he felt it was the greatest ever done on the screen. Director Paul Bern felt that Clara was potentially the greatest dramatic actress of her day, who could play demanding emotional roles.

The public, however, called for Madcap Clara, the It Girl, and Clara responded by filling the role on screen and off. Down Wilshire Boulevard she would fly in her flaming red Kissel convertible, surrounded by seven auburn chow dogs chosen to match her hair. Clara herself would take the wheel. She had no plans to hire a chauffeur, she told the world; she couldn't find one who would drive fast enough.

From time to time, she reverted to roller skates, arriving at the Paramount lot in a state of flushed excitement. She had brought her father west and set him up in a dry-cleaning business. After gathering up Paramount employees' dirty clothes, she would skate off with the bundles, headed for her father's store.

As a star Clara did not forget her tomboy days, when she had played baseball and football with the boys. To her house in Hollywood she invited the entire University of Southern California football team for a midnight practice session on the lawn. The team, the famous Thundering Herd, liked it and came again. While All-American tackle Jesse Hibbs was showing Clara an end-around play, Clara landed on her own end and sprained a thumb. Later there was talk of a romance with Hibbs, quickly denied, but then there was talk of romance the minute Clara reached Hollywood.

"You'd trust her with your life, your money, your reputation, but certainly not with your husband," wrote the journalists, eager to make her as sirenic as her screen image. In these efforts she often cooperated. When a young man sang his love under her window, she listened, amused. The suitor, a former Yale football player, persisted, and when Clara remained indifferent, he slashed his wrists in a suicide attempt. Given a sanity hearing, he was released after he told the court that Clara had kissed him so forcefully that his jaw ached for days. Her comment was basically a lesson in etiquette: "Men don't commit suicide by slashing their wrists. They use pistols."

She was similarly caustic when she learned from newspapers that her marriage to leading man Donald Keith was set. "But why not?" she chirped, apparently content to let the press play matchmaker. Her name was linked with Keith's until her attentions shifted to Gilbert Roland, who, like Keith, had appeared with her in *The Plastic Age*. The two saw each other regularly for more than a year. Both were temperamental, independent, jealous. Working on different sets with attractive partners brought on strains and quarrels. The affair broke up.

Clara wasted little time before announcing her engagement to director Victor Fleming, considerably older than she. Never a great reader, under his influence she took to books, to music, to art. In the long run, culture didn't take. Incompatibilities in age and temperament led to a friendly parting.

The tabloids were happy when lanky Gary Cooper, a former Nevada cowpoke, stepped into the breach. After a small part in a western he played with Clara in *Children of Divorce*. His ardent pursuit reflected his prairie vitality, but the accompanying jealousy was of the classic, unbending variety. It helped to end the romance, although not before headlines milked each detail of the good times and the bad.

Bela Lugosi, Nino Martino, John Gilbert, and others were linked with Clara, but the man who dominated her life for several years was debonair Harry Richman, radio and recording star, owner of a New York night club. Month after month, millions read that Richman and Clara were engaged, not engaged, had set the wedding date, had canceled the wedding date, were more in love than ever, had broken off for good.

In New York actress Flo Stanley threatened to sue Clara for alienating Richman's affections. "Harry's my man," she declared. "He doesn't love that little kid. He's only playing with her for the publicity he can get out of it." Richman had a different view. Clara was his because other men did not appreciate her. "They petted her too much," he said. "I understand her as a woman. They only understood her as an artist."

Clara candidly added her view of the relationship. "I'm not sure I really know what love is all about. When I get married, I want it to last." A little later she reflected, "If there's such a thing as love, then I'm in love with Harry Richman." Richman may have put a quietus on the romance by saying, "Clara needs a man about the house—someone to tell her what to do." Said Clara in definitive reply, "I've always had my own way, and I always will."

Malicious tongues found ample occasion to wag after Clara went to the hospital for an appendectomy. The surgeon in attendance was William Earl Pearson, whom she had met while filming on location in Dallas. As the doctor-patient relationship grew more intimate, the press as usual took note. So did the doctor's wife, who brought suit for alienation of affections.

To reporters in Dallas, Clara said: "He told me that he had just been married and that he and his wife were always squabbling and didn't understand each other. I never had had a date with a married man in my life, and I wouldn't have had dates with this one if he had had any kids, but of course he didn't. And do you know what happened next? The wife sued me for 150,000 smackers for alienation of affection. Blam! Like that. One hundred and fifty thousand smackers! Why, I never had seen that much money before." Clara admitted she had settled out of court for $30,000. Henceforth she would be "real quiet and orderly."

"If I could only find the right man, someone who would give me something," she said in assessment of her lengthening list of loved and lost. "I'm unhappy, desolate. My mind goes on even when my body sleeps. I've always given. I've had no children. My mother's illness. Her horrible death. The demands that have always been made upon me. But I could be happy, I believe, if I could find the right man."

The search continued. "The trouble with boyfriends is that they all want to make you over into something else again," she complained. "It burns me up, especially as it's me as I am that they fall for." The more she saw of men, she added, the better she liked dogs.

Her love for one man was enduring. Sometimes Clara told friends that her purpose in life was to make Robert Bow happy. After his laundry business failed, she set him up in a restaurant, which likewise was unsuccessful. Other ventures did poorly, but Clara didn't really mind. When she engaged a secretary in 1928, her father promptly fell in love and married her. The move brought happiness to the couple. Later, however, another girl replaced Clara's step-mother and led Clara into a disastrous court battle that helped to end her halcyon days in Hollywood.

For the moment her career was still in full flower, although the edges of the blossom were beginning almost imperceptibly to wilt, the product to grow stale. In a departure from type, she made *Wings* in 1927. William Wellman directed this impressive study of aviators and their lives and loves during World War I. Charles "Buddy" Rogers, Richard Arlen, and Gary Cooper were in the cast. For once, Clara was not the It Girl, carelessly vamping men, but a more complex, rounded personality. Her performance was engaging, and it carried depth.

Clara was back at the old stand in *Get Your Man*, a thin French farce with Charles Rogers and Josephine Dunn; in *Roughhouse Rosie*, where she danced the Charleston and the Black Bottom; and in *Hula*, which the *New York Times* called a "helpless hodgepodge." The year 1928 saw her carry on in *Ladies of the Mob, Red Hair, The Fleet's In,* with comedian Jack Oakie, and *Three Week Ends.* "These stories of chaste dancing girls in waterfront halls have to be handled in a wonderfully expert fashion to interest even the younger lads and lasses," warned a critic.

Richard Watts, Jr., wrote at this time about star personalities, how they became the pets of exhibitors, their films tailored so that each mannerism, each weakness even has to be evident in a constant repetitive flow. In the case of Clara Bow, he elaborated: "Because this delectable young star happens to be an alluring, dashing little flapper, whose exuberant charms demonstrate the happiest features of the highly publicized jazz spirit, all of her vehicles must overrun with self-consciously youthful gaiety. . . . Because she has had the misfortune to be labeled the It Girl, she must turn out to be a sort of Northwest Mounted Policeman of sex, who gets her man if she has to bludgeon him. The result of all this is a series of films in which a particularly engaging star gets coy and roguish and fiendishly elfin all over the landscape, battering down the resistance of some man who, for an unaccountable reason, is cold to her loveliness, and with all the force of her go-getting instincts, overthrowing the unfortunate and helpless rival who opposes her. Of course, she walks off with this hero in the last reel. This formula is inherently one of the most annoying on display . . . but it is particularly boring when applied to one of the most pleasing stars of the cinema, a player who in such pictures as *Mantrap* and *Dancing Mothers* proved that she is one of the real actresses of the screen."

"When they line up a story for me, the first thing they think of is: how do we get Clara undressed?" said Clara. To add to her troubles, sound was coming in. In the matter of voice, she had little to worry about. Hers was passably pleasant, low, and throaty. The difficulty lay in the restrictions the microphone put on movement. One of her greatest fortes was animal energy, kinetic enthusiasm that kept her in constant motion. Now she often heard the director shout, "Cut, we're not picking you up, Clara." Annoyed, she would rush to kick the mike, but with sound techniques still primitive, it stayed where it was, confining her high spirits to its immediate area, cramping her style.

The production machine at Paramount continued its grueling pace. Clara made *The Saturday Night Kid*, with Jean Harlow in a bit part and Jean Arthur in a major role. On first hearing her voice, Jean Arthur wailed, "A foghorn," and ran from the recording studio. The foghorn quality turned out to be one of her greatest assets. In *The Saturday Night Kid* there were critics who felt she stole the picture from its star.

Clara went on to do a specialty number in *Paramount on Parade*, which also featured Maurice Chevalier, Ruth Chatterton, William Powell, and Mitzi Green. She made *Love Among the Millionaires*, *Kick In*, and *The Wild Party*. Charles Ruggles and Skeets Gallagher played with her in *Her Wedding Night*, and Fredric March appeared as a sailor who won her heart in *True to the Navy*.

Often the schedule dictated an eighteen-hour day. Demanding song-and-dance numbers were run through again and again to reach the desired performance level. With microphone fright, now a maddening phobia, added to other tensions, Clara ate nervously, adding pounds that made her five-foot-three frame plump rather than voluptuous.

"Get up in the morning—go to work," she complained. "Work, work, work. Go home at night. Can't sleep. Think too much. Think about everything. Mind goes on and on and on. Think about my life, about the new picture, about my lines. Is that living? To hell with it. What's life? This isn't it. . . . My nerves are all shot. I'm at the breaking point."

After her father moved out to live with his bride, Clara was lonely. She invited her new secretary, Daisy DeVoe, to live in. Her house, in Beverly Hills, was modest—seven rooms in one story set far back on a broad lawn, the style Spanish adobe, the path to the front door lined with rose trees. Contrasting with expensive tapestries and oil paintings in other stars' homes, Clara's furnishings cost less than $25,000, less than some extravagant bathtubs alone. Pola Negri, Mae Murray, and Gloria

Swanson gave elaborate parties, but Clara liked to play poker with her household servants. Cops on the beat always knew that the back door was open, the refrigerator stocked with beer and sandwiches. Others entertained visiting royalty, but Clara's small beach house at Malibu usually played host to prop boys and extras.

Similarly, travel and clothes meant little to the It Girl. Clara's favorite outfit consisted of a skirt, a sweater, and a pair of low-heeled shoes. She wore slacks for a change of pace at a time when they were not yet fashionable. In ten years the only traveling she did was a short trip to Agua Caliente and another to New York, playing pinochle all along the route with her secretary. There was only one unusual preference that Clara indulged, much to the amusement of visitors to the Bow home. A Persian rug had been carefully tailored to fit not the living room floor but the bottom of the swimming pool.

Beneath the apparently giddy life, the heady stardom, Clara remained essentially a frightened child, puzzled by life. "I always want to cry," she said at the peak of her popularity. "I could cry any minute." To ward off disturbing thoughts a phonograph played continuously in the house; loud dance music could be heard day and night. On a table by the bed a regiment of bottles contained pep pills and sedatives.

Nervous breakdowns began to take their toll years earlier. During the filming of *Roughhouse Rosie*, late in 1926, Clara suffered a mild collapse. "It was because she couldn't decide between Gary Cooper and Victor Fleming. We had to shut down the picture for two weeks," said its director.

After that the breakdowns kept coming. Clara went on working, but as emotional and professional pressures increased, the illnesses drew closer together. "Even now, with all I see before me, I cannot quite trust life," she told Adela Rogers St. Johns. "It did too many awful things to me in my youth. I still feel that I must beat it, grab everything quickly, enjoy the moment to the utmost, because tomorrow life may bludgeon me down as it did my mother, as it used to do to the people I lived with in Brooklyn when I was a kid."

Late in 1930 came a minor but distasteful incident. The press reported that Clara had welched on gambling debts incurred at the Calneva Lodge in Lake Tahoe. Checks for losses bore her name, were countersigned Daisy DeVoe, but came back later with the notation, "Payment stopped." Clara denied the resort's claims, adding that she always paid legitimate debts promptly. When the dispute continued to draw attention, she gave out a statement:

> While I was at Lake Tahoe, Mr. Will Rogers invited Rex Bell, my secretary, Miss DeVoe, and myself to dinner. I did not know the hotel was a gambling place until after we reached there. After we had dinner, Mr. Rogers went to one of the gambling tables, and naturally we went with him. I began to play a little at a game called "21," which they call there Black Jack. They gave me 50-cent pieces to play with, and I signed some checks in blank, telling the dealer to fill in the amount of the 50-cent pieces he had given me. There were four checks. It now seems they claim these 50-cent pieces represent what they call $100 chips and they put enough in the checks to amount to that. When the checks reached my bank, they called me and said the checks had a slip on them asking the bank to "wire fate of these checks." This attracted the attention of my banker, and I found out for the first time this gambling house claimed I had lost and owed them nearly $14,000, so I told the bank not to pay the checks.

While the dispute was settled amicably, damage was done to Clara's reputation. Nothing, however, could compare to the blow about to fall. After a brief stay at a Glendale sanitarium Clara returned to her old routine of filmmaking and a troubled life in Beverly Hills. One night a dispute at the end of a poker game erupted into violent argument with secretary Daisy DeVoe. So heated did charges become that Clara fired the girl, whom she considered her best friend. When the press learned of the incident, Clara said, "I had a perfectly good reason for discharging her. It was a personal reason, and I can't say what it was."

On November 14, Daisy began unloosing public accusations against her former employer-companion. She had a verbal contract that still had three years to go, she said, and her attorney was checking into this. She had been discharged because a new man in Clara's life had succeeded in "muscling" her out of a job. "He is supposed to be a big, manly man, but it was certainly a dirty trick he did to me," Daisy explained. The new figure in Clara's life was known to be handsome cowboy star Rex Bell. His role in the affair added relish to mounting gossip. It was revealed that he had accompanied police officers when they opened Daisy's bank deposit box. Jewelry and other items belonging to Clara were uncovered. Daisy had later been grilled by the police investigators.

On November 15, Los Angeles County District Attorney Fitts said that Daisy DeVoe, former private secretary to Clara Bow, had signed a thirty-page statement confessing to the theft of $35,000 in cash and property. It left him no alternative, he said, but to put the matter before a grand jury. From Daisy's attorney, Nathan Freedman, came word that she would deny the alleged confession and file a damage suit against Fitts's office for unjustly keeping her in custody.

Clara herself refused to sign a complaint. However, the action she and Bell had initiated was not easily curtailed. After hearing both her and Daisy, the grand jury returned an indictment citing thirty-five counts of grand theft.

Amid a blaze of publicity, the trial of Daisy DeVoe opened on January 13, 1931, before a packed Los Angeles courtroom. Clara made her entrance escorted by Rex Bell, her wavy red hair hidden under a tan felt hat. Before Superior Court Judge William Doran she testified that she had employed Daisy, her onetime hairdresser at Paramount, as her secretary in January, 1929. She paid her $75 a week, a salary that had not changed.

"How did she leave your employ?" asked Assistant District Attorney David Clark, who was handling the case.

"She just left," Clara replied.

"What were her duties?"

"All she had to do was to pay my bills and take her salary checks out of the Clara Bow special bank account."

"Did you ever authorize her to make checks out of that account to herself other than her salary?"

"Never did."

The prosecution thereupon produced thirty-seven checks listed in the indictment. He asked Clara if she had authorized them.

"I should say not," she said.

As she answered, she caught the eye of the young defendant, a cool, composed blonde. "All right, go ahead and sneer at me, Daisy," she said. When Daisy turned away, Clara reached for a handkerchief and dabbed at her eyes.

A few moments later she gave way to tears. She was asked about Daisy's purchase of a silver dresser set. She said that Daisy had given it to her on her birthday. Only later did she learn that it had been out of the Clara Bow account. "I thought she was being sweet and kind," Clara sobbed. "She was my friend—the only friend I had in the world. I'm sorry I'm crying. I can't help it."

She continued to be teary-eyed when she was questioned at length about a check for $825, with which Daisy was said to have bought a beige fur coat. "Did you sign this check, Miss Bow?" she was asked.

"Certainly, that is my check," she replied. "I signed it myself, but Miss DeVoe brought it to me and said it was to go in my income tax. I signed it because I trusted her."

The item was later to prove a decisive factor in the case.

Clara's testimony ended the day in court. When the second session opened the next morning, the prosecution put before the jury the thirty-page statement that Daisy had made the previous November. In it she allegedly admitted demanding $125,000 from Clara to keep quiet about "things I know."

"What do you know?" Chief Investigator Blayney Matthews had asked her.

"I think it would be to her advantage to keep my mouth shut," Daisy had replied.

"And for things that you know you demanded $125,000?" Blayney persisted.

"Yes," Daisy purportedly said.

A key to the alleged extortion attempt—in which, the document showed, Daisy had not persisted—was the personal correspondence of Clara Bow. "Clara kept heaps of love letters," said one excerpt from the statement. "One time I burned all that had accumulated from various men for two years. I burned all of Gary Cooper's. Clara got very sore and quarreled with me for three days because I burned them, but I knew the letters might get her into trouble some time."

While Cooper's letters had been destroyed, Daisy had salvaged and taken love notes from men who signed themselves Earl, Harry, and Rex. These were introduced as evidence.

Later in the document Daisy stated that she had started embezzling from her employer in 1929. "Yes, it's so hard to see a girl like Clara with everything and no respect for anything," read the testimony. "It was her fault. If she had paid attention to business, I wouldn't have taken a dime from her because she would have known it. She wouldn't even write her own checks. She put me in a position to take everything I wanted. Of course, I didn't blame her."

The statement revealed that Daisy had bought clothing and jewelry for herself and a ring for a male acquaintance, made payments on her mother's house and auto, and helped a sister financially. "I was going to tell Clara about it later on," she said. "I couldn't see my mother lose her home and everything. I made five or six payments on the house and car."

One of the things that Daisy had noted was Clara's financial relationship with Robert Bow. "Clara told me that her father ran through $25,000 of her money, and she was keeping his canceled checks in case he tried to make trouble for her," the statement read.

Also included was an account of Daisy's discharge, which she laid at the feet of Rex Bell. The transcribed notes said that Daisy had heard Clara talking to Bell about the matter. "I don't care," Daisy recalled Clara as saying. "If you want her to go, Rex, you can tell her yourself, because I won't tell her."

"Did you notify Miss Bow that you were about to leave?" investigator Matthews had asked. The transcribed reply created an uproar in the courtroom.

"No, because Miss Bow was drunk, and if I had gotten into

Clara Bow

Child actress Clara Bow in *Down to the Sea in Ships,* 1922.

Clara Bow and co-star Ernest Torrence in *Mantrap,* 1926. Audiences began to realize then that she had IT.

Clara Bow with new leading man Gary Cooper in *Children of Divorce*, 1927. The death scene in *Children* brought Clara to the attention of director Victor Fleming.

"She radiates an elfin sensuousness," said the *Times*. Here Clara plays a love scene with Charles "Buddy" Rogers.

Clara Bow in her history-making nude swimming scene in *Hula* (1927),
directed by Victor Fleming.

Clara as Hula Calhoun and co-star
in *Hula*.

Clara and Antonio Moreno in Elinor Glyn's *It*, 1927.

Dangerous Curves, 1929, added to Clara's extensive popularity.

Clara made *The Saturday Night Kid* (1929) with Jean Harlow (center) in a bit part and Jean Arthur (right) in a major role.

Love Among the Millionaires, a 1930 Paramount production, with Stanley Smith.

Left: Frederic March and Clara in *True to the Navy* (1930).

Paramount on Parade, 1930, featured Clara, Skeets Gallagher (left), and Jack Oakie.

Top: Regis Toomey and Clara cling to each other in *Kick In,* 1931.

Left: Clara in *Love Among the Millionaires.*

Clara poses for publicity during the Daisy DeVoe larceny trial.

Clara Bow and Rex Bell.

Clara and her daughter-in-law, Mrs. George Bell, at the funeral of Rex Bell.

any argument with her, she would have tried to kill me, because she had tried to once before and I wouldn't have any words with her at all," read Daisy's answer. "I thought it would be better to walk out and later on straighten out her affairs. I wanted to get things settled as quickly as possible to keep Clara out of the papers, because one more slam in the papers and Clara is through in pictures."

After the reading of the lengthy statement, Clara was recalled to the witness stand for cross-examination. Defense attorney Freedman moved quickly to establish Bell's role in the affair.

"As a matter of fact, Bell discharged Miss DeVoe, didn't he?" he asked.

"He didn't. I fired her myself because she wasn't honest," Clara snapped.

"Well, he's your secretary now, isn't he?" Freedman continued.

"He is not. I know it has been printed that he is, but it is not the truth."

"Doesn't Bell live on Bedford Drive?"

"How dare you!" Clara exclaimed.

Clara's attorney, W.I. Gilbert, testified briefly that Daisy had come to him to ask for $125,000. If she didn't get the money, she had said she would turn information about Clara "over to newspapers."

Clara recalled that after the meeting with Gilbert, Daisy had nevertheless come to her and asked for her old job back. When Clara had accused her of demanding the money, Daisy had admitted it. "Yes, my best friend, that was the way she answered me," Clara said on the stand, dabbing her face with a powder puff. "I said, 'Listen, Daisy, are you kidding me? After all the money you have stolen from me, and after trying to get $125,000 out of me for the return of my letters and telegrams, you want your job back?"

Prosecutor Clark disclosed that 147 canceled checks, representing withdrawals from the Clara Bow account, were missing. He alleged that on the dates of withdrawal Daisy had deposited similar amounts to her own account. Over her 22 months of employment, these deposits totalled $19,872. While more might have been embezzled, he was resting his case on the 35 checks that the alleged confession by Daisy had enumerated. These totalled $16,000.

The prosecution next identified diamond rings, watches, and an ermine coat, all taken from the defendant's safe deposit box, plus a coat taken from the home of her sister. Investigator Marjorie Fairchild was asked to repeat what Daisy had said when the jewelry and other items, allegedly Clara's, were recovered. "She said she could not stand seeing her family go without things when Miss Bow had so much and was so reckless with money," she recalled. "She said at first she had not taken anything, but after seeing the actress so reckless it seemed unfair, and taking things seemed easy."

With this testimony the prosecution rested its case. Daisy DeVoe was the first scheduled defense witness. "I haven't told anything yet," she said shortly before the court convened. "I've lied and lied to protect Clara Bow, and I'm not going to now. I've got to tell the truth for self-protection, no matter how it hurts her."

When Daisy DeVoe took the witness stand, Clara was not in the courtroom. The defense counsel began by challenging the validity of Daisy's alleged confession. Declaring that it had been obtained by third-degree methods, counsel asked for a dismissal of all charges. When the court denied the motion, Daisy began her testimony. She seemed eager to tell of her life as attendant to a great star. She described her secretarial duties in Clara's household.

"I was to take care of all bills and not bother her with them," she began. "I was to write all checks, make payments on the mortgage on her house and lot, pay all salaries, including my own and that of her father, pay all of Clara's liquor bills, and buy all her clothes." With a wry smile, she added, "I also bleached and hennaed Clara's hair and took the lines out of her face so she would look good before a camera."

"Did you act as her companion as well as her secretary?" attorney Freedman asked.

"Yes, and when I first went with her, she said that after she had dismissed the chauffeur, I could make myself available to drive the car around."

"What were your duties as Miss Bow's companion?"

"I went with Clara everywhere, and I would go to the door when various men arrived and tell them she was at home or not at home, according to her wishes."

Questioned about finances, Daisy said she would sometimes get behind in her $75 weekly salary and therefore make out checks to herself to catch up. On other occasions, she would take her own money to pay bills at the door, later reimbursing herself by check.

"What did you pay for Miss Bow at the door?" asked Freedman.

"Liquor. Much liquor."

"What was the most you ever paid for liquor at one time for Miss Bow?"

"I don't know exactly. I think it was about $275."

"Did you have access to her account before you moved into Miss Bow's home?"

"Yes, to the special Clara Bow account."

"Did you ever have occasion to pay poker debts?" Freedman pursued.

"Oh, yes, lots of times. We played poker nearly every night. She liked to play poker, and we'd stay home as many as six nights a week just to play it when she wasn't working in pictures."

Asked if her employer had her buy jewelry, Daisy said: "I made so many trips to the jewelers I don't remember them all."

"Name some of them."

"I bought a watch and chain for Dr. Earl Pearson. I paid around $4,000 for it. I bought a star sapphire ring for Lothar Mendez for $900. I bought an engagement ring for Miss Bow for $10,000. I bought a watch for Harry Richman for $2,000."

Returning to the matter of household money affairs, Daisy's counsel asked her to elaborate on her role and Clara's attitude.

"Whenever she would find me at work on the check stubs,

she would grab them and strew them on the floor," Daisy said with a slight pout. "She would tell me there were other things she wanted me to do, and not to waste time on such foolishness."

Asked about the beige coat costing $825, Daisy said that she had bought it and written a check for it, but at Clara's request. "I took it to Clara's house," she added. Mr. Rex Bell wouldn't let me in." Thereafter, she had taken all the articles Clara had entrusted to her care, put them in a suitcase, and taken them to the home of her sister.

The day's testimony concluded with Daisy's denial that she had embezzled money from her employer. With the witness turned over to the prosecution, the court adjourned for the weekend.

On Saturday afternoon the ailing Clara propped herself up in bed and talked to reporters, holding court in her Beverly Hills home. Lifting a hand to her forehead, she pushed back the tangled red curls. "Look at the roots," she said angrily, "Why, that hair was red when I was born, had been red ever since, and is red now and always will be. Of course, I did have to put some henna on it. It was too dark for red, and I had to brighten it up for the camera."

That pressing matter disposed of, Clara discussed the beginnings of the feud with her secretary. "Things got worse on my trip to New York last year," she recalled, her voice hoarse due to bronchitis. "One of my maids called my attention to the fact that Daisy's clothes cost more than mine and that her wardrobe was much classier. As a result, I looked into the money matter, and soon it was all over."

As to the liquor purchased by her ex-employee, Clara had a simple answer. "Oh, she took lots of it home," she explained. "She played poker, too, every time I did. And she lost, too."

Clara's voice began to give out. She answered several technical questions, and the interview was terminated. "And don't forget this either," she shouted after the parting reporters. "Daisy's hair is bleached!"

Meanwhile, Daisy was holding her own press conference,

telling news reporters that she had much yet to tell, "about drinking parties and escapades." "I am not trying to make a scandal out of anything I know about Clara," she said, "but I have to tell these things if I expect to defend myself successfully against the charges she has caused to be brought against me."

Judge William Doran took note of the sideline kibitzing. When the court reopened on Monday, January 19, he set up judicial ground rules. "The defendant in this case is charged with grand theft and has pleaded not guilty," he declared. "The issue here is clear cut. The question is: Did she steal the money? I have in mind that this issue should not be met by generalities and indirections but by specific proofs. Reading the accounts of this trial in the newspapers, the public might well be in doubt as to who is on trial."

The next day Alfred Mathes took the stand. A curly-haired youth whom Daisy had met through Rex Bell, he testified that many of the things Daisy had bought out of the actress's funds were purchased at Clara's request. Others who took the stand for Daisy were her sister, one of Clara's dressmakers, and several tradespeople.

The dressmaker told of the day she was in the Bow home when Daisy told Clara, "My own checking account is over-drawn, and what am I going to use for money?" Clara had said, "I don't want you to let your account get like that, Daisy. You draw enough out of my account to make up the amount and take $300 more."

Frances Blair, a former maid, testified that she heard Daisy ask Clara several times to reimburse her for money that she had spent for her.

Daisy returned to the stand to assert that it was her own financial knowledge that had built up Clara's fortune. When she had become her secretary, in January, 1929, the Bow bank account had been a mere $30,000.

"And how much did she have in her trust fund when you left last November?" attorney Freedman asked.

"She had $227,000 in it," Daisy answered.

Assistant District Attorney Clark made the state's summation, flaying the defense for raising smokescreen generalities to cover direct evidence of theft. Turning to the defendant, he said that she had plotted deliberately to get everything she could. She had learned that she would be discharged. "She then went out and bought a lot of things," he went on. "She paid all of her outstanding bills with Miss Bow's money. Then she got hold of the canceled checks and the actress's love letters—the one to hide because she knew that if it was found it would reveal her guilt, and the other to use as a blackjack on the actress if her action should be discovered."

When the sensational news of the alleged theft appeared in the newspapers, Clark said, Daisy tried to hush it up. "She went to W.I. Gilbert, Miss Bow's attorney, and demanded $125,000 or she would give the love letters to the papers and tell about her life with Clara. It was blackmail, and what a picture Miss DeVoe saw in her mind—the love letters of a famous actress on the front pages."

The final picture that emerged, the prosecutor concluded, was of Clara Bow, "an artist with no business sense," and Daisy DeVoe, "a girl who betrayed a trust." He asked for a verdict of guilty on all counts.

"They were like sisters, these two," Nathan Freedman began in his summation for the defense. "Clara said, 'Daisy, what is mine is yours.' How could this little girl keep the accounts straight, no matter how she tried? Can't you hear Clara say to Daisy DeVoe, "Come on, baby, let's go places and do things.' And then she would grab a couple of checks, and away they would go. Please, I ask you to understand as humans." When, in closing, Freedman pictured the defendant as a "misguided girl, perhaps, but one who would do no intentional wrong," Daisy, until then perfectly composed, cried softly.

In his charge to the jury, the judge explained that they must return separate verdicts on each of the thirty-five counts and that their decisions must be unanimous. Punishment was one to ten years on each count, a possible total of 350 years in prison if convicted on all counts. After going into a brief legal explanation of the relationship of servant and employer, Judge Doran told the panel of seven men and five women that they must be positive "beyond reasonable doubt" if they found the defendant guilty.

While the jurors retired to deliberate her fate, Daisy remained in the courtroom, surrounded by friends. "I have faith. . . I feel sure they will free me," she said. Her accuser, Clara Bow, remained bedridden at home from the continued effects of a heavy cold and nervous strain.

Not until Friday, January 23, did the jurors come to a decision. After two days of deliberation they brought in a verdict of guilty of one of the thirty-five counts, item 7 of the indictment. The jury concluded that Daisy got Clara to sign a blank check, presumably to pay for an income tax installment, but in reality to buy herself an $825 fur coat. A request for leniency was added. On the other thirty-four counts the defendant was found not guilty.

Photographers used a new type of flashbulb near Daisy to get her reaction to the verdict. It was the spark that touched off nerves strained during the ten difficult days in the court. The twenty-six-year-old defendant sobbed convulsively and threw herself into the arms of her sister. "If they were going to convict me at all, why didn't they convict me of everything," she cried before bailiffs took her away to the county jail for the night. Three of the five women jurors cried openly, and others in the courtroom wept in sympathy for the convicted girl.

Still at home in bed, Clara was not happy with the verdict. "I am terribly sorry all this had to happen," she said. "For Daisy's sake I hope the court will be lenient." Several days later she sent a letter in her own handwriting to the court, saying that she would not have prosecuted if her former employee had not threatened to blackmail her. "I find myself unable to avoid letting you know that it is my hope that mercy will be shown to Daisy DeVoe," she wrote.

"Clara's ways are not my ways," Daisy countered. "I would rather not comment on anything Miss Bow does. It's nice enough for her to write the letter, but it must be remembered that if Clara Bow had thought a little more before she started all this, it would not have happened." Daisy continued to put much of the blame for Clara's conduct on Rex Bell, whose contract, she maintained, had just expired at the studio, and who wanted her job. He had convinced Clara that she was stealing, when in actuality Clara had approved of her purchases of clothes and automobiles, knowing full well they could not be bought on a salary of $75 a week.

On February 16 sentence was finally pronounced. Judge Doran put Daisy on probation for five years, with the provision that she spend eighteen months in the county jail. "The evidence was sufficient to return a conviction on all counts," he added. Daisy's attorneys began a long series of appeals, during the course of which she served most of the term imposed.

Shortly after the trial the publisher of a West Coast weekly was arrested, charged with sending through the mails obscene literature purporting to reveal the intimate life of Clara Bow.

Clara herself withdrew to a secluded sanitarium, where she received treatments to assist her recovery from a complete nervous breakdown. Peggy Shannon, a recent addition to the New York stage, replaced her in a scheduled new picture. At the same time *No Limit*, Clara's last film preceding the trial, opened its run in the nation's theaters. "Miss Bow may survive the DeVoe trial, but she can hardly survive pictures like *No Limit*," said the *New York Herald Tribune* of the shopworn effort.

"There is no question that the girl, who for two years, in my opinion, was the greatest actress on the screen, is in poor physical condition, and there is a big chance she will never make another picture," said B.P. Schulberg from his office as production manager of Paramount. "It was one of the most tragic things I have ever witnessed, that hearing. Clara has the biggest heart in the world and now, because of her kindness to others, she confronts termination of her really great career."

Several weeks later, at Clara's request, she was released from her contract. She left the sanitarium for the Nevada ranch of Rex Bell.

"The trouble with me is, I'm no sneak," she said, recalling

the trial. "Why, I've never done a thing that everybody else in Hollywood hasn't done. I may have made mistakes. I certainly must have been foolish. But my greatest mistake seems to have been that I was open and aboveboard about everything."

Today the love notes that Clara received from admirers seem tame, almost tepid. Their notoriety at the time was great. They were addressed to the It Girl. Clara Bow, the personification of the postwar flapper, was supposed to be rebellious and alluring, bewitching and wild, even naughty—but basically nice. There was the rub. Clara had not only flirted; she had obviously given in to her suitors. The It Girl had become the Id Girl, someone said.

Clara had good reason to be annoyed by the sudden upsurge of public puritanism. For the better part of a careless decade fans had adored her antics, lived vicariously through her see-sawing romances. What she could not have foreseen, however, was the 1929 Wall Street debacle. With it the gay twenties gave way to the gray thirties. Things that had seemed funny and acceptable turned sour and silly. The spirit of the times had passed by the girl with the heart-shaped face, whose publicity posters once ballyhooed her as "Spirit . . . a living symbol of our idols, speed and pep."

Weary, double-chinned from a sudden spurt in weight, her eyes betraying hurt, Clara bleached her hair blonde and roughed it on the ranch in Nevada. On December 4, 1931, she was married to Rex Bell by a Las Vegas justice of the peace. After a European trip the couple alternated between the ranch and Hollywood. Bell opened a sporting goods store and became active in Nevada politics. Clara returned to work and made two films, *Hoopla* and *Call Her Savage*, in which previously modest breasts grew to surprising proportions in an effort to keep up with the changing national taste. Neither film was a success. With Bell, Clara opened the It Café on Hollywood's North Vine Street. It failed.

A son was born to the couple in 1935 and another in 1938. "I don't want my two boys to become Hollywood kids. I wouldn't want them to go through what I did," Clara told reporters who popped in from time to time at the sprawling, isolated ranch in Nevada.

Far from the pressures of Hollywood, she regained her figure but not her health. The sleepless nights jarred a constitution she had abused over the years. "Maybe I can't sleep because I'm trying to discover who Clara Bow is, who she was—and who she's got to be," she assessed her own difficulties.

As the nervous condition grew worse, psychiatrists were called in to help the tomboy from Brooklyn who had become the incandescent symbol of a reckless age. Their efforts held her illness in check but produced no cure. Trips to sanitariums became routine. By the end of the forties there was talk of trouble between Clara and her husband, but it was quickly denied. "We've never discussed divorce," Bell told news reporters and referred in passing to his wife's last public appearance, as Mrs. Hush, the "mystery voice," on a 1947 "Truth or Consequences" show. "She might not say so to anyone, but I believe that it means something to her that after this many years people still ask about her."

In 1954 Bell was elected lieutenant-governor of Nevada, and in 1956 he gave an interview to Bob Thomas, in which he admitted that his wife was now an emotional invalid. "She has had to live an entirely different life since the trouble began," he said. "She needs the constant care of a doctor and must go to a sanitarium when her condition gets worse. That's why she must stay in Los Angeles; we don't have the facilities here in Nevada. She has been down there for the past four years. Some of the time she spends in a sanitarium in Culver City; we also have an apartment nearby. I get down every four or six weeks and our sons visit her when they can. . . . Unfortunately, she doesn't have a bit of social life. That's one of the things she can't take in her condition. If she had been Minnie Zilch instead of Clara Bow, perhaps this would never have happened to her. But the emotional strain of her early years was just too much for her nervous system. It's like training horses. Sometimes when you're starting thoroughbreds, you break them in too early, while you take a saddle-horse and bring him along easy."

In July, 1962, Bell, a candidate for governor of Nevada, died of a heart attack after attending a Republican Fourth of July rally in Las Vegas. Fifteen minutes before the funeral services began, on July 9, a small sedan drove up beside the Forest Lawn Church of the Recessional in Glendale, California. Bent by grief but smiling wanly, Clara Bow stepped out to make her first appearance in public in ten years. A wide-brimmed hat, dark glasses, and a black silk dress formed her mourning costume. Her two sons escorted her into the church. When the brief ceremony was over, she returned to the car and to her life of seclusion.

Friends said that at home she lived with a nurse, filling her days with swimming and reading, her great preference being for fan magazines. She also liked to watch television, and occasionally she sent notes to the performers she admired, fan letters much like those she had received in her heyday at the rate of 40,000 a week.

It was the nights that were most difficult. The small radio under her pillow played soft music to induce sleep, but often the device failed. After bouts of melancholy Clara would retreat to the sanitarium high in the Hollywood hills. There she would pace nervously back and forth, waiting for the darkness to fall. From the window she could see the distant outlines of several of the giant film studios. "It wasn't ever like I thought it was going to be. It was always a disappointment to me," she said.

Still, it was to that fabled world of make-believe that she retreated each night. Her nurse was sitting with her watching the "Late Late Show" on September 27, 1965, when she saw Clara stiffen suddenly and lose consciousness. A heart attack brought peace to the restless spirit of the once-famed It Girl.

"We did as we pleased," she had often remarked in her later years when describing the time of her greatest triumphs. She had forgotten, perhaps, that there was less spontaneity than rebellion, less joy than anxiety in her willful actions. Despite her jaunty, self-confident air, Clara was often at a loss, whether on the grimy side streets of Brooklyn or on the palm-lined boulevards of a fast-paced Hollywood.

At her death, Whitney Bolton recalled the long ago day when he had come up to her on the side of a Paramount stage and asked, "Miss Bow, when you add it all up, what is It?" After a moment's hesitation, Clara had looked up and said, with the candor so characteristic of her, "I ain't real sure." Clara Bow was never real sure.

 CONCLUSION

Other sirens, other vampires, figured in the early days of silent films. Valeska Suratt lured men to destruction at Theda Bara's own studio, Fox, while devilish Louise Glaum, known as the Spider Woman, vamped for Triangle Productions in a gown of black velvet and jet spider webs. Both fell from popularity in the postwar film slump in the early twenties.

In the second wave of vampires that succeeded these pioneers, Pola Negri and Barbara LaMarr figured prominently, along with Dagmar Godowsky and Nita Naldi. Dagmar, daughter of famed concert pianist Leopold Godowsky, became known as the Snake Woman, who supposedly shed her skin every spring. With her black hair parted in the middle and drawn smoothly down to the neck, the slinky star hissed her way through a sizable series of films. In 1958 she wrote *First Person Plural*, a delightful autobiography, in which she confessed that in later life she had lost virtually everything except weight, tipping the scales at startlingly unsnakelike figures. Clearly, she had also lost her old status, for early in the game Theda Bara had laid down a dictum: no fat vampires.

195

From a New Jersey convent to the chorus line at the Winter Garden led the road traveled by tall, dark, beautiful Donna Dooley. Her dancing and heroically proportioned bust attracted the attention of John Barrymore, who found a part for her in his film version of *Dr. Jekyll and Mr. Hyde.* In Hollywood the alchemy of press agentry transformed Donna into Nita Naldi and rhapsodized her as a patrician grande dame, daughter of a famed Italian diplomat and distant relation of Dante's Beatrice. In more than forty films, such as *Glimpses of the Moon, You Can't Fool Your Wife, The Unfair Sex*, and *Lawful Larceny*, Nita stole other men's wives. In *Blood and Sand, Cobra*, and *A Sainted Devil* she co-starred with Rudolph Valentino.

"The fans just assumed that I was in real life as I appeared on the screen. Women loathed me," Nita said in an interview as she recalled her Hollywood stardom. "I was warned not to appear on the public beaches, and everywhere I went people used to look upon me as something unreal—like griffins and unicorns."

As the talkies took over, Nita retired from films to marry J. Searle Barclay, a millionaire who later lost his money and died intestate. After his death her career was limited to occasional Broadway roles and television appearances. Penniless, nearly blind as the result of an affliction she blamed on the aluminum reflectors of old movie sets, the former vamp was also plagued by a heart ailment. The Actor's Fund paid part of the rent for her small single room in New York's Times Square area. Here she still received old friends, sometimes greeting them with gifts, mementos of her days of triumph. One who came often was John Barrymore's daughter, Diana, who called her Mother Moonbeam. There were no callers after February 17, 1961, the day a maid found Nita Naldi's lifeless body on her hotel bed. Death came from a heart attack.

None of the five stars treated in this book successfully survived the advent of talking pictures. Greta Garbo's first American films, *Torrent, The Temptress*, and *Flesh and the Devil*, proved that she could smoulder and lure with the best of the silent seducers, and her later career established her as one of the all-time greats of the talkies. The enigmatic Swedish player's life has been covered in a number of books and is not given treatment here. Nor is space devoted to talkie stars Jean Harlow, Marlene Dietrich, and Mae West, or to other sex goddesses closer to our own era, such as Marilyn Monroe and Hedy Lamarr, who has written a scorching account of her own life and loves, male and female.

In the silent era encompassed by these pages there is one other actress, however, whose career deserves mention: Lya De Putti, the midnight beauty who succeeded to Pola Negri's throne when Pola left Europe for the United States. Born in Hungary of an aristocratic family, Lya's adventuresome nature led her to the circus, a nunnery, and a dancing vaudeville chorus. A German director liked her expressive face—the large, dark eyes, the delicate nose and mouth, the hair trimmed neatly like a boy's. For the UFA studio in Berlin she made *Jealousy, Young Blood*, and *Manon Lescaut*. She eventually was known as the German Theda Bara.

Hollywood imported Lya, as it had Pola Negri before her. Publicists saw to it that tantalizing tales, albeit false, were circulated about her, including one that said she left Hungary in 1918, when the Rumanians were driven out, and went to Bucharest, where she was arrested and sentenced to death as a Hungarian spy before friends smuggled her away to safety.

For her first American film Lya was cast in D.W. Griffith's *Sorrows of Satan*, and her performance was favorably reviewed. However, subsequent efforts, in *The Prince of Tempters, The Heart Thief*, and other trite vampire epics, failed to catch fire. The disillusioned Lya was only thirty-two on November 26, 1931, when she died, of double pneumonia in New York City.

While it was known that she had been briefly married to a Swedish diplomatic attaché and later to a high official of the Hungarian judiciary, from whom she was divorced, a singular set of events transpired at Lya's death. First, her divorced husband committed suicide, attributing his act to financial reverses. His friends, however, regarded this as a fiction devised to hide the great tragedy of his life, the loss of Lya to the stage and screen. Before their parting Lya had borne him two daughters, it was revealed. At his death, these two teenage girls learned for the first time the identity of their mother, whom they had long thought dead. After the divorce from Lya, the father had placed a stone over an empty grave, its inscription reading, "Lya De Putti Died 1920." Over the years he had intercepted all messages from Lya to the children and had regularly taken them to place flowers near her tombstone.

Only a handful of mourners attended Lya's funeral services in New York. All arrangements were handled by a Hungarian woman, whom the newspapers described as "the actress's secretary and intimate friend." There was subtle irony—but also some logic—in the fact that another vampire, presumably dedicated to luring men, had felt the need for close companionship from her own sex.

When she was practicing mass-seduction of America's males, Clara Bow looked on her female secretary as a kindred spirit. Late in life Pola Negri found the presence of a compatible woman a continuing comfort. Vampires, after all, formed a type of sisterhood. And as Theda Bara had said, there was something of the kleptomaniac in most of them, the desire to take what was not theirs, really a poor basis for harmonious relationships with men. Just as well, perhaps; it was less dangerous to stick to their own kind.

While their insecurity intensified with success, many of the silent screen sex goddesses were unsure of themselves and puzzled by life from the very start. Perhaps this very instability drove them to seek reassurance in screen images of smouldering sensuality, of desirability.

Barbara LaMarr, reared by foster parents, longed for someone to call her own. When men failed to meet her needs, she adopted a baby, repeating the pattern of her own existence. Mae Murray's parents left her with a grandmother, who in turn put her into convents and boarding schools. Like Barbara, she later found it difficult to evaluate people, to understand their subtleties, to be close to them. Tomboy Clara Bow, roaming the streets of Brooklyn, saw that life could be hard, and she never completely trusted it. Pola Negri lost her father at an early age but always retained the image of a strong beloved figure. Through an endless carousel of love affairs, she continued her search for that ideal man whom she never really knew, who was hopeless to replace. More prosaically, Theda Bara was reared in a middle-class family, which remained together even during the days of her greatest fame. Only she managed to escape the emotional turbulence which characterized her peers. For the other love goddesses in this book, love could be very confusing indeed.

 FILMOGRAPHIES

Films of THEDA BARA

A Fool There Was 1915
The Clemenceau Case 1915
The Devil's Daughter 1915
Lady Audley's Secret 1915
The Two Orphans 1915
Sin 1915
The Galley Slave 1915
Destruction 1915
Carmen 1915
The Serpent 1916
Gold and the Woman 1916
The Eternal Sappho 1916
East Lynne 1916
Her Double Life 1916
Romeo and Juliet 1916
Under Two Flags 1916
Fires of Hate 1916
The Vixen 1916
The Tiger Woman 1916
Darling of Paris 1916
Camille 1917

Madame DuBarry 1917
Her Greatest Love 1917
Heart and Soul 1917
The Rose of Blood 1917
The Soul of Buddha 1917
Cleopatra 1917
Salome 1918
Under the Yoke 1918
The Forbidden Path 1918
When a Woman Sins 1918
The She Devil 1918
The Light 1918
The Message of the Lillies 1918
La Belle Russe 1918
Siren's Song 1918
When Men Desire 1918
A Woman There Was 1919
Lure of Ambition 1919
Kathleen Mavourneen 1919
The Unchastened Woman 1925
Madame Mystery 1925

Films of BARBARA LAMARR

Paying the Piper 1921
The Desperate Trail 1921
The Nut 1921
The Three Musketeers 1921
The Prisoner of Zenda 1922
Arabian Love 1922
Trifling Women 1922
Quincy Adams Sawyer 1922
Poor Men's Wives 1923
Souls for Sale 1923
The Brass Bottle 1923

Strangers of the Night 1923
The Eternal Struggle 1923
The Eternal City 1924
Thy Name Is Woman 1924
The Shooting of Dan McGrew
    1924
The White Moth 1924
Sandra 1924
The Heart of a Siren 1925
The White Monkey 1925
The Girl from Montmartre 1926

Films of POLA NEGRI

The Yellow Ticket 1918
Passion 1920
Gypsy Blood 1921
One Arabian Night 1921
Vendetta 1921
The Last Payment 1922
The Red Peacock 1922
The Polish Dancer 1922
The Eyes of the Mummy 1922
Mad Love 1923
Bella Donna 1923
Passion 1923
The Cheat 1923
The Spanish Dancer 1923
Shadows of Paris 1924
Men 1924
Lily of the Dust 1924
Forbidden Paradise 1924
East of Suez 1925
The Charmer 1925

Flower of the Night 1925
A Woman of the World 1925
Crown of Lies 1926
Good and Naughty 1926
Hotel Imperial 1927
Barbed Wire 1927
The Woman on Trial 1927
The Secret Hour 1928
Three Sinners 1928
Loves of an Actress 1928
The Woman from Moscow 1928
Are Women to Blame? 1928
Forbidden Paradise 1929
The Woman He Scorned 1930
A Woman Commands 1932
Fanatisme 1934
Mazurka 1935
Madame Bovary 1937
Hi Diddle Diddle 1943
The Moonspinners 1964

Films of MAE MURRAY

To Have and to Hold 1916	*Twin Pawns* 1919
Sweet Kitty Bellairs 1916	*A.B.C. of Love* 1919
Honor Thy Name 1916	*On with the Dance* 1920
The Dream Girl 1916	*The Right to Love* 1920
The Big Sister 1916	*Idols of Clay* 1920
The Plow Girl 1916	*The Gilded Lily* 1921
On Record 1917	*Peacock Alley* 1921
A Mormon Maid 1917	*Fascination* 1922
The Primrose Ring 1917	*Broadway Rose* 1922
At First Sight 1917	*Jazzmania* 1923
The Princess Virtue 1917	*The French Doll* 1923
Face Value 1918	*Fashion Row* 1924
The Bride's Awakening 1918	*Mademoiselle Midnight* 1924
Her Body in Bond 1918	*Circe the Enchantress* 1924
Modern Love 1918	*The Merry Widow* 1925
Danger—Go Slow 1918	*The Masked Bride* 1925
The Scarlet Shadow 1919	*Valencia* 1926
What Am I Bid? 1919	*Altars of Desire* 1927
Big Little Person 1919	*High Stakes* 1931
The Delicious Little Devil 1919	*Bachelor Apartment* 1931

Films of CLARA BOW

Down to the Sea in Ships 1923
Enemies of Women 1923
Black Oxen 1924
Maytime 1924
Poisoned Paradise 1924
This Woman 1924
Grit 1924
Capital Punishment 1925
Eve's Lover 1925
Kiss Me Again 1925
The Keeper of the Bees 1925
The Best Bad Man 1925
The Boomerang 1925
Free to Love 1925
The Great Sensation 1925
Dancing Mothers 1926
The Runaway 1926
Mantrap 1926
The Plastic Age 1926
Kid Boots 1926
It 1927

Children of Divorce 1927
Roughhouse Rosie 1927
Wings 1927
Hula 1927
Get Your Man 1927
Red Hair 1928
Ladies of the Mob 1928
The Fleet's In 1928
Three Week Ends 1928
The Wild Party 1929
Dangerous Curves 1929
The Saturday Night Kid 1929
Paramount on Parade 1930
True to the Navy 1930
Love Among the Millionaires 1930
Her Wedding Night 1930
No Limit 1931
Kick In 1931
Call Her Savage 1932
Hoopla 1933

1 2 3 4 5 6 7 ← P Y → 9 8 7 6 5 4 3